GENESIS to REVELATION

MATTHEW

ROBERT E. LUCCOCK

PARTICIPANT

GENESIS to REVELATION

MATTHEW

ROBERT E. LUCCOCK

PARTICIPANT

GENESIS TO REVELATION SERIES: **MATTHEW**
PARTICIPANT

ISBN 978-1-501-84841-4

Manufactured in the United States of America

17 18 19 20 21 22 23 24 25 26—10 9 8 7 6 5 4 3 2 1

ABINGDON PRESS
Nashville

TABLE OF CONTENTS

"They will call him Immanuel"
(which means "God with us") (1:23).

1

JESUS' BIRTH, INFANCY, AND BAPTISM

Matthew 1–3

DIMENSION ONE: WHAT DOES THE BIBLE SAY?

Answer these questions by reading Matthew 1

1. With whom does the genealogy of Jesus begin? (1:2)

2. What five women are included? (1:3, 5, 6, 16)

3. Is the ancestry traced to Joseph or Mary? (1:16)

4. How many generations are reported? (1:17)

5. What are the major divisions in the ancestry? (1:17)

6. Why does Joseph first want to divorce Mary? (1:18)

7. What does the name *Jesus* signify? (1:21)

Answer these questions by reading Matthew 2

8. Who is the king of Judea when Jesus is born? (2:1)

9. How do the magi (wise men) know that Jesus is to be born in Bethlehem? (2:5-6)

10. Why don't the magi return to Herod? (2:12)

11. Why does Joseph take the family to Egypt? (2:13)

12. Whom does Herod kill in Bethlehem? (2:16)

13. Where does Joseph take Jesus and Mary when they return from Egypt? (2:21-23)

Answer these questions by reading Matthew 3

14. What message does John the Baptist preach? (3:2)

15. Who foretells that a preacher will "prepare the way for the Lord"? (3:3)

JESUS' BIRTH, INFANCY, AND BAPTISM

16. Where do the people come from who want to be baptized by John? (3:5)

17. Whom does John call a "brood of vipers"? (3:7)

18. What does John tell them to do? (3:8)

19. Why does John first refuse to baptize Jesus? (3:14)

20. Why does Jesus say it is fitting for John to baptize him? (3:15)

21. What does Jesus see when he is baptized? (3:16)

22. What does the voice from heaven say? (3:17)

DIMENSION TWO: WHAT DOES THE BIBLE MEAN?

The first two chapters of Matthew tell of Jesus' ancestry and birth and the flight into Egypt. These stories, like the ones in Luke 1–2, were told to report the wonderful and miraculous things people believed happened at the birth of the Messiah.

Chapter 3 is the account of John the Baptist's preaching and Jesus' baptism by John. Jesus emerges onto the public scene of his ministry here.

■ **Matthew 1:1-17.** How could Matthew introduce such an important book with a column of genealogy? Finding a more boring beginning for any book, especially this one, is hard to imagine. Let's imagine ourselves back in time to the first-century church of Jewish Christians for whom Matthew writes. Now does it sound boring? Far from it. In fact Matthew can scarcely have chosen a better way to begin. This report of Jesus' ancestry was written for the Jews who have chosen to follow Christ. It tells them that the history of God's salvation began with Israel in the covenant God made with Abraham. This salvation comes directly down to "Jesus who is called the Messiah" (1:16). The former covenants are not broken. On the contrary, Christ's followers inherit the promises once made to Abraham, Isaac, Jacob, and David. This genealogy is not written to persuade anyone to believe in Jesus as the Christ. Matthew's Christians already believed that. The genealogy links their new experience with Israel's salvation history.

If we think about this list of sometimes unpronounceable names we may wonder about three things. Three groups of fourteen generations each are listed. We do not know why the list is composed the way it is. But Matthew clearly divides the ancestry by three of the greatest names and events of Israel's covenant history. The list goes on from Abraham to David, from David to the Babylonian Exile, from the Exile to Jesus.

Matthew was way ahead of his time by giving five women as much place as this in God's design for salvation.

And why does this genealogy trace the ancestry to Joseph if he is not the genetic father of Jesus? According to the tradition, Jesus was the son of Joseph's virgin wife. Apparently this inconsistency does not trouble Matthew. Jesus can descend from Abraham and David and forty others and still be born without any blood connections (as we understand it) to Joseph.

■ **Matthew 1:18-24.** Betrothal—the pledge to marry—was more binding then than engagement is to us now. Mary already was considered to belong to Joseph in betrothal. He wants to divorce her quietly, to hurt her as little as possible.

He must have been baffled by his dream. But he trusts the Lord's word. Incidentally, God uses dreams five times in the first two chapters. These dreams insure that God's divine purpose is not frustrated and Jesus' safety is assured.

The names given to Mary and Joseph's child are important. They foreshadow what the whole Gospel will proclaim. Actually, these names are profound theological statements: *Jesus*, the way of salvation from sin; *Immanuel*, the incarnation of God with us.

■ **Matthew 2.** What an incredible surprise that the Christ should be born unannounced. And Matthew implies in his Gospel that leaders of Israel failed their watching and waiting. Should they have been more attentive?

The rising star (2:2) is Matthew's way of saying that the very heavens marked the birth of Immanuel. This birth was truly a cosmic event. Divine guidance is given to those who would come to worship and pay homage.

"[Herod] was disturbed" (verse 3). His rage and cruelty (verses 16-18) show how Jesus threatens all entrenched worldly power. The Herods are one of the most monstrous families history has ever seen. One of Herod's sons torments Jesus at his trial and adds his power to the forces that brought Jesus to his death (Luke 23:6-15a).

Matthew quotes the Old Testament four times in Chapter 2 (verses 5, 15, 17, 23) and once in Chapter 3 to account for what happens to the infant Jesus. Matthew refers to the Old Testament as a device. He declares that the salvation history of the Jews is preparation for fulfillment in Christ. God's promise is unbroken from Abraham to the present.

■ **Matthew 3:1-12.** For John to call these people a "brood of vipers" when they come to be baptized seems rude. He denounces them as snakes. This implies that they are descended from the great snake, Satan himself. John believed piety without repentance was a great sin. John saw this unrepentant piety in these people.

If we read verses 7-12 carefully, we hear three themes that Jesus will later repeat. The first theme used by John is the denunciation of the Pharisees and Sadducees. In Chapter 23, we will find Jesus raising the same indignation that John first sounds here. The second theme used by John also uses the metaphor "every tree that does not produce good fruit" (verse 10). Jesus speaks these very words in the Sermon on the Mount (7:19). In 12:33-34, Jesus even uses the phrase "brood of vipers."

The third theme used by John (3:12) and later picked up and developed by Jesus is the separation of wheat and chaff. Jesus brings this theme to its fullest development in the disconcerting parables of the last judgment in Chapter 25. John the Baptist, blunt and frightening, may not be anyone we would like to invite home to Sunday dinner. But even this brief appearance leaves no doubt how important he was in preparing the way of Jesus.

■ **Matthew 3:13-17.** Why would Jesus come to be baptized? Certainly not because he had sins that needed to be washed away. And surely he was not there to be baptized as a disciple of John. Jesus was there because all Israel was called to this baptism. Ordinarily Jews were not baptized, except persons who converted from another faith. But here the whole nation was called to a cleansing. They had fallen so far from fidelity to the covenant they needed to begin as fresh converts. Jesus understood that he was required to identify with God's people altogether. His baptism was a way to "fulfill all righteousness," of doing what God asked of this whole nation.

Who saw the Spirit descending like a dove (3:16)? The voice, "This is my Son, whom I love," is seemingly spoken only to Jesus. Those words, taken from Psalm 2:7 and Isaiah 42:1, make an unmistakable claim about Jesus. No one would think of quoting those passages unless in reference to the Messiah. Everything that follows in the whole Gospel takes its course from this claim.

We have learned in these three chapters that Jesus is the Christ (Messiah). This fulfills all the earlier covenants between God and Israel. This Messiah will save God's people from the power of their sins. In him, God has come to be with the people of the covenant. Jesus has come to call people to bear the good fruit befitting repentance.

DIMENSION THREE: WHAT DOES THE BIBLE MEAN TO ME?

Sometimes we receive correspondence that closes with the familiar letters *R.S.V.P.* ("please reply"). The Gospels are communications with an R.S.V.P. both at the end and posted throughout. What do we find in these chapters that seems to be an R.S.V.P. for us? We should ponder at least the following three things: a genealogy, a murder, and a call to repent.

Matthew 1:1-17—Genealogy From Abraham to Jesus

Forty-two generations stretch between Abraham and Jesus. If we count four generations to a century, then eighty of our ancestors lie between Jesus' life and ourselves. Think carefully about that—just eighty people in a human chain reaching across the centuries. No one traces their ancestry back to Jesus. And spiritual ancestry can come through those who stand outside direct descent to us. But to consider the eighty who have gone before us in an unbroken line is reason for thanksgiving.

Matthew gives us forty-two names. Some of these people were notable persons in history. Most of them were ordinary people. They provide the transmission line from Abraham to Jesus. How much we owe to their faithfulness and courage! And the debt goes on to the eighty who have joined the line since Jesus. Who were the persons who are our ancestors? What did they endure? In what ways can we be thankful for their existence? Thank God for ordinary people. None of them were perfect, but without them we would not be where and what we are.

Matthew 2:16-18—Murder

Have you ever thought of those innocent children dying because they happened to be born within two years of Jesus' birth? Evil incarnate in the murder of children! And how much suffering, inexplicable and unjustified, the world has witnessed. Let us beware of finding easy answers to evil, or even any answers at all. Perhaps the whole Gospel of Matthew will help us find ways of dealing with it. Can faith help to see us through? Can we ignore the stories in the Bible that tell of evil and suffering? How do we deal with stories about child abuse and the sexual exploitation of children?

Matthew 3:2, 8—Fruit That Befits Repentance

Can we imagine John the Baptist preaching any differently today? And why should he? John looked around at the lives of those who came out in "repentance." He failed to see any fruit commensurate with their penitence. He failed to see any fruit that corresponded to the sins of which they were supposedly repenting. Would he see us any differently? If people have defrauded the innocent, they need to repay. If out of fear they have refused to act when the times called for decision, they need to pray for courage. If they have harbored grudges in anger when reconciliation could have taken place, they need to go and be reconciled. What kind of fruit might befit the repentance we need?

Jesus began to preach, "Repent,
for the kingdom of heaven has come near" (4:17).

TEMPTATIONS, THE SERMON ON THE MOUNT
Matthew 4–5

DIMENSION ONE: WHAT DOES THE BIBLE SAY?

Answer these questions by reading Matthew 4

1. Where do the temptations of Jesus occur? (4:1)

2. How long do the temptations last? (4:2)

3. What is the first temptation? (4:3)

4. Why does Jesus resist the first temptation? (4:4)

5. What is the second temptation? (4:5-6)

6. Why does Jesus resist the second temptation? (4:7)

7. What does the devil promise Jesus with the third temptation? (4:8-9)

8. What is the third temptation? (4:8-9)

9. Why does Jesus resist the third temptation? (4:10)

10. When does Jesus return to Galilee? (4:12)

11. Where does Jesus go to live in Galilee? (4:13)

12. How does Jesus begin his preaching? (4:17)

13. What two sets of brothers does Jesus call? (4:18-21)

14. What does Jesus do as he goes about Galilee? (4:23)

Answer these questions by reading Matthew 5

15. Where is Jesus when he gives this sermon, and to whom is he speaking? (5:1)

16. How many beatitudes does he speak? (5:1-11)

17. Which beatitude does Jesus address to the disciples? (5:11)

18. Why are the disciples told to let their light shine? (5:16)

19. What inner attitude does Jesus say makes a person subject to judgment? (5:22)

20. How does Jesus say one can commit adultery? (5:28)

21. According to Matthew, does Jesus permit divorce on any grounds? (5:32)

22. How are Jesus' followers to be? (5:48)

DIMENSION TWO: WHAT DOES THE BIBLE MEAN?

■ **Matthew 4:1-2.** What an abrupt contrast from the uplifting brightness of Jesus' baptism to the threatening shadows of the temptation! The Spirit moves with Jesus from one event to the other (3:16; 4:1). Jesus sees the Spirit descending on him at his baptism. The Spirit then leads him "at once" (Mark 1:12) into temptation. Why? Why would God's Holy Spirit lead Jesus into temptation?

■ **Matthew 4:1-11.** For one thing, when we use the word *temptation* we generally mean "to entice to commit some immoral act." But *temptation* here is more like "testing." And is it not essential that Jesus test his call and his baptism as the beloved Son? As the Christ, he will face many opportunities to use his power in ways that would deny God's purposes. The temptations are really a testing of Jesus' obedience to God and how he will use the gift of the power of his Sonship.

We can better understand what the three temptations mean to Jesus by looking at his replies to the devil. To the temptation to turn stones into bread Jesus responds, "Man shall not live on bread alone, but on every word that comes from the mouth of God." Jesus is hungry in that scorching desert. He feels in his hunger the terrible hunger of the world. He remembers the hunger of the Israelites during the Exodus. He then recalls God's word to them (Deuteronomy 8:3). These words are crucial for Jesus now. A full stomach is not enough.

Jesus answers the temptation to perform a sign (4:5) by telling the devil, "Do not put the Lord your God to the test" (Deuteronomy 6:16). The Israelites, while wandering in the desert, tested God to prove the covenant promises (Exodus 17:1-7). This Jesus will not do.

To the temptation to worship the devil, Jesus quotes Deuteronomy 6:13-14. This verse is really a restatement of the first commandment. If Jesus gave his allegiance to the devil, even if he thereby gained the whole world, it would not be for God. He would in the end lose both his soul and the kingdoms of the world.

Under the old covenant, Israel was frequently called God's Son (Hosea 11:1). Now Jesus hears himself called Son of God. Remembering the failure of Israel's faith long before, Jesus must not fail these same tests as God's beloved Son. The devil was an opposing spirit, one who tempts persons to do evil and thus thwarts God's will. When Jesus dismisses him (4:10) he calls him Satan.

■ **Matthew 4:12a, 17.** Some events have an effect on history far beyond the moment the event happens. Caesar crossed the Rubicon; Roman history took a new course. Fifty-six men in Philadelphia, in 1776, signed a Declaration of Independence. The whole world has changed. Herod arrested

John the Baptist and set forces in motion that turned the world upside down. According to Christian faith, Jesus' preaching, which began when John was arrested, signaled the near approach of a kingdom that would alter the face of affairs on earth. Verses 12 and 17 mark a decisive turning point not only for Israel, but for the world.

■ **Matthew 4:13-16.** But why did Jesus begin in Galilee? Galilee had an enormous population. One of the great highways of the ancient world ran through Galilee. It carried the influence of that world into Israel. Galilee was probably the most fertile field for the gospel in Palestine. Moreover, it was heavily Gentile in its racial and ethnic make-up. Matthew frequently emphasizes the universal appeal of the gospel. Galilee was a natural beginning place.

■ **Matthew 4:17.** Jesus and John both make a promise (the kingdom of God is fast approaching) and a demand (repent).

■ **Matthew 4:18-21.** Simon (Peter) and Andrew, and James and John stand out among the Twelve. We see and hear them more than any of the others. Were they waiting for Jesus' call? Was Jesus so compelling that they left everything at once "and followed him"? Simon, Andrew, James, and John were ordinary men. We do not have any record that they were morally bad at the time they were called. Jesus calls those persons who are morally upright as well as Matthew the tax collector whose morals are questionable.

■ **Matthew 4:23-25.** In these three verses, Matthew summarizes the whole ministry of Jesus. Jesus is proclaiming the good news of the Kingdom. He is instructing the congregations in their synagogues. And he is restoring people to health.

■ **Matthew 5.** We call this the Sermon on the Mount although it is not really a sermon but a collection of the sayings of Jesus. Matthew has arranged them carefully. They form the finest summary of Christian morality found anywhere. He speaks to the disciples. This chapter contains the following five distinct blocks of material: nine beatitudes or blessings (5:2-12); a brief discourse on righteousness and the law (verses 17-20); a formula of contrast between the old interpretation of the law and the new, applied to six moral questions (verses 21-47); and the admonition to "be perfect" (verse 48).

■ **Matthew 5:2-12.** Studying the Beatitudes can mean a lifetime of learning. An hour or two of study every now and then can only open the way to our continuing engagement with their truth. These nine verses have sometimes been badly mishandled in preaching and private devotion. They have either been suffocated with sentimental piety or we have heard them as impossible demands and incredible claims. The Beatitudes are exclamations of joy. The believer will find the blessing (happiness, grace—no one English word will do it) from the promise of the Beatitudes. Many translations properly punctuate the Beatitudes with exclamation points. These exclamation points may be a good key to unlock the meaning of the words they punctuate.

In 4:17, Jesus announces, "The kingdom of heaven has come near." According to Matthew, the next words we hear from Jesus (omitting the personal call to Peter and Andrew) are those of the first beatitude. "Blessed are the poor in spirit, for theirs is the kingdom of heaven." The kingdom of heaven ties the good news of Jesus' proclamation to the promise of the Beatitudes. In the kingdom of heaven one shall have the blessings promised in these verses. One who believes the gospel and has put his or her heart under God's rules knows beatitude. Right now! These blessings are not just good moral wisdom thrown out to the crowd. They are descriptions of what life is like for those who have heard and believed the good news of God's promises in Jesus the Christ.

■ **Matthew 5:13.** As future leaders of the movement, the disciples' salt would be needed, just as salt is essential to preserving food and for enhancing taste.

■ **Matthew 5:14-16.** Someone once said, "There can be no such thing as secret discipleship, for either secrecy destroys discipleship (lamp under a bushel), or discipleship destroys the secrecy (lamp on a stand)."

■ **Matthew 5:21-48.** Jesus repeats the formula "You have heard that it was said to the people long ago. . . . But I tell you . . ." six times. In each case Jesus drives the issue inward to a person's will and soul, where sin comes from. Anger precedes murder. Lust comes before adultery. Our behavior toward others comes out of the attitudes and feelings we have toward them in our souls. Nourishing and giving hospitality to anger breeds hatred. Having these feelings toward another person violates that person. The scribes and Pharisees refrain from murder. The disciples must refuse to embrace anger and hatred. Their righteousness must exceed that of the Pharisees. The "I tell you" could only be spoken by one whose authority comes from God.

■ **Matthew 5:48.** The word *perfect* in New Testament Greek (*teleios*) is never used to mean "moral perfection." It conveys the idea of the fulfillment of the purposes that we accept because we love and serve God. We are to strive to realize God's purpose for us. Of course, no one can claim moral perfection. But we can accept fully the end God has for each of us.

DIMENSION THREE: WHAT DOES THE BIBLE MEAN TO ME?

Matthew 4:1-11—Temptation

Dramatic and vivid as this story may be, what meaning can it have for us? None of us is the Son of God like Jesus. Nor are we tempted to perform miracles or test God by jumping off buildings. And no one ever promised us even a rose garden, let alone all the kingdoms of the world. So these are not our temptations. Ah, but perhaps Satan wants us to think just that. As long as we think of turning stones into bread, leaping from the temple, and worshiping the devil we may not wake up to the power struggle going on in every one of us. Jesus was being tested to see how he would use the Spirit. But every person baptized and confirmed in Christ receives the gift of God's Spirit, however difficult it may be to feel it. With that Spirit comes a testing: how will we use the gift of God's Spirit?

What gifts do we have? Some of them are mentioned in Galatians 5:22. Others may be the charisma of a strong personality, the communication skills of a good teacher, the charity and cunning of an effective public servant, and so forth. These gifts can be abused as well as used for holy purposes. To what disposition or loyalty do you release your gifts? How could you be tempted to use your gifts of the Spirit to an evil end?

Matthew 5:2-12—The Beatitudes

Try reading the Beatitudes as plain descriptions of "how things are." Forget who said them or their context for a moment. When we read that way some of them are hard to believe. Since when is mourning a blessing? Ask someone in mourning if he or she feels blessed. The meek inherit the earth? They are more likely to be trampled by the aggressors, aren't they?

But read them now with the assurance that God's kingdom already has drawn near. Remember the words of Matthew 28:20: "I am with you always." The person who believes in Jesus finds in God's living presence a grace that transfigures the poverty or peacemaking of every day. I am blessed when I mourn for the sin and sadness and death in the world, as God in Christ weeps over our world. Why? Because, in such mourning, I come close enough to feel something of the divine pathos. So, says Jesus, you will neither need nor desire further reward. The joy of being, living, and doing in the Spirit of God's purposes and care reinforces us. It gives us strength to meet the assault of the evil that lies in wait for God's obedient servants. What difference does the awareness of God's presence in our midst make when we face the tragedies of our life?

The class may discuss this topic if time allows.

Matthew 5:21-47—The Higher Righteousness

Can we imagine any one of us never getting angry, never feeling a lustful impulse, never having the desire for revenge? What can we really make of these extravagant commands? We may start with the recognition that anger, images of sensuous desire, and the urge to retaliate come to everyone. The point is not that we feel these things. The point is whether we give them room and allow them into our imagination. That is what makes the difference. How can one evil thought begin to multiply? Have we ever brooded about something until we got even more worked up? How can we keep from having thoughts that Jesus would disapprove of?

Seek first his kingdom and his righteousness (6:33).

THE SERMON ON THE MOUNT

Matthew 6–7

DIMENSION ONE: WHAT DOES THE BIBLE SAY?

Answer these questions by reading Matthew 6

1. What does Jesus warn his disciples against? (6:1)

2. Of what three forms of piety does Jesus speak? (6:2, 5, 16)

3. What does Jesus call people who make a show of their religion? (6:2, 5, 16)

4. What does Jesus say these people receive? (6:2, 5, 16)

5. With what three petitions about God does Jesus' prayer begin? (6:9-10)

6. What three things does Jesus ask for? (6:11-13)

7. What does Jesus tell his hearers about "treasures" and how to deal with them? (6:19-21)

8. Why does Jesus say we cannot serve God and money? (6:24)

9. What three things does Jesus warn us not to worry about? (6:25, 31)

10. Why does Jesus say we should look at the birds? (6:26)

11. Why does Jesus tell us to consider the flowers of the field? (6:28-29)

12. Instead of worrying, what does Jesus say we are to do? (6:33)

Answer these questions by reading Matthew 7

13. If we who are evil know how to give good gifts to our children, what does God do? (7:11)

14. How should we treat others? (7:12)

15. How will the disciples know the true prophets from false prophets? (7:16)

16. Who will enter the kingdom of heaven? (7:21)

17. What is the person like who hears Jesus' words and puts them into practice? (7:24)

18. What is a person like who hears Jesus' words and does not put them into practice? (7:26)

19. Why were the crowds amazed at Jesus' teaching? (7:29)

DIMENSION TWO: WHAT DOES THE BIBLE MEAN?

The twenty-six–mile course of the Boston Marathon passes through the city of Newton. In Newton, between miles sixteen and twenty-two, the runners have to climb four hills. These hills are so demanding of stamina and physical and mental commitment that the final hill is called Heartbreak Hill. This hill usually determines who will finish the course. Chapter 6 is the middle chapter of the Sermon on the Mount. This chapter might well be called the Heartbreak Hill of Jesus' teaching, at least in this sermon. This chapter is challenging and uncompromising in its demands. This chapter settles whether anyone attempting the course of Christian faith and life has the stamina to stay with it. In the words of Jesus, which Matthew brings together here, the stress is on undivided loyalty and commitment.

The chapter contrasts five sets of opposites: false and true piety, treasures on earth and in heaven, darkness and light, money and God, anxiety and seeking the kingdom of heaven. Jesus allows no compromise between each of these alternatives. The problem the sermon was first addressed to is the fantasy that people can have it both ways. The sermon still speaks to this issue. In a manner of speaking it is heartbreaking to discover that we cannot have it both ways.

■ **Matthew 6:2-4, 5-6, 16-18.** In this three-verse poem, Jesus compares the piety of hypocrites with the devotion appropriate to his disciples. In each case, in giving alms to needy persons, in prayer, and in fasting, the difference lies in motivation. Why do we give alms, pray, or fast? Do we pray to be seen and praised by others, or to please and worship God? Or, do we hope to enjoy the publicity and worship at the same time? In the practice of devotion there is no choice between God and persons. It is all for God. Jesus calls for uncompromising devotion to God.

Almsgiving to help the poor and needy was the supreme act of piety in Jewish practice. The rabbis said, "Greater is he who gives alms than he who offers all sacrifices." The temptation was great to practice this piety ostentatiously to reap the praises of others. Jesus calls such people hypocrites. These wear masks to hide their insincere or mixed motives.

"They have received their reward in full" means that they already have the praise of people. The people's praise is what these pious people want. The people's praise is what they get. God's blessing is not part of the bargain. Pretentious public prayers are the same. Jesus is not opposed to synagogue prayers. Jesus calls for prayers to be humbly uttered. The same is also true with exhibitionist fasting. True piety is practiced in secret where what we do and say is known only to God. Jesus does not say what reward shall be given. Judging from the rest of the Gospel, however, the reward is the

GENESIS to REVELATION **MATTHEW**

beatitude that comes from doing God's will. Jesus never promises special privilege or honor, even to his disciples.

■ **Matthew 6:7-13.** This passage contains a prayer for Christian disciples. It assumes that the kingdom of heaven is near (4:17) and that God will save the people from their sins (1:21). These are the great promises of the gospel.

Jesus gives his disciples a model of prayer. We are to pray like this. Notice that the first three petitions concern God (the Kingdom, hallowing the Name, God's will). The final three requests concern ourselves (bread, forgiveness, deliverance from the evil one). The final doxology, "For yours is the kingdom and the power and the glory forever. Amen," is a later addition.

■ **Matthew 6:24-34.** We must understand what these verses are really all about. Jesus is not counseling us to be shiftless or improvident. Nor are these words mocking the troubled poor, not knowing if they will gain life's necessities. *Worry*, in these verses, means being anxious, or distracted by cares that are full of fear. Worrying is being preoccupied with obsessive concern for food, clothes, and the things everyone needs. God's purpose and will are kept aside. Keep in mind, Jesus speaks here to his disciples. They are about to go out not knowing how they will live. Jesus certainly does not expect that they can just stand outside and life's necessities will fall on them. But he tells them not to worry or be bothered by necessities. They are to seek God's kingdom first. The rule of God's Spirit should be in all that they do. This counsel is not for those with little faith (6:30).

■ **Matthew 7:1-5.** Do not judge? But I have to judge. I'm buying a car. Do I not have to judge whether the dealer tells the truth? I'm a teacher. I must judge whether a student has cheated. I'm a parent. May I not judge the honesty of what my child reports? A hundred times a day we have to judge and make moral judgments. But Jesus' words are not about moral neutrality. Verses 3-5 make his meaning clear. Look first at the plank in your own eye before pointing to the speck in someone else's eye. This warning is against judging with severe self-righteousness.

■ **Matthew 7:6.** Applying these expressions to Gentiles and tax collectors would be contrary to the attitude of Jesus toward them. Are Gentiles and tax collectors not the very ones to whom Jesus has been sent? Yes, but Jesus means what he says here. He has a reason to say it. For the gospel to be heard the persons to whom it is spoken must receive it. They must be open and teachable. Those with minds already made up, the soil of their spirits like rocky ground (13:5), are the hard-hearted. They will trample the holy and attack those who speak what they will not or cannot receive.

■ **Matthew 7:7-11.** In Luke 11:5-13, this passage on prayer follows the Lord's Prayer. The passage in Luke is interrupted only by the short parable on the importunity of the friend at midnight. That seems the more logical order. Jesus here is lifting the morale of his threatened disciples. He is arming them with the strong assurance of the power of prayer. The promise in Matthew 21:21-22 echoes the pledge here in Chapter 7.

■ **Matthew 7:12.** The first-century rabbi Hillel is attributed with another form of this rule. He said, "What is hateful to you, do not do to your neighbor." Because one would be refraining from what is hateful, wouldn't this negative summons be easier to obey? But Jesus' words say in positive principle what the Last Judgment (25:31-46) says in parable. Behind this rule is the conviction that what God has done to and for us, so we are to do to and for each other.

■ **Matthew 7:13-27.** The final verses of the Sermon on the Mount contain wisdom and warnings about false prophets, false prayers, and false foundations. These form a short primer for Christian disciples. Later (10:16), as Jesus sends his disciples out, he reminds them to be as shrewd as snakes. These verses spell out the unassailable reasons why that wisdom is needed.

■ **Matthew 7:28-29.** Throughout the Sermon on the Mount we have assumed that Jesus speaks here to his disciples. We assume that both because of what it says in Matthew 5:1 and because of the pointed instruction that obviously has the disciples in mind. But here we read that the crowds are astonished. It might be that Jesus speaks publicly to his disciples when they draw near. The point Matthew makes is that Jesus spoke with his own authority. Only the Messiah could do that!

DIMENSION THREE: WHAT DOES THE BIBLE MEAN TO ME?

Matthew 6:25-34—Worry and Seeking the Kingdom

This statement seems at first reading to be about as unrealistic as anyone can get. In a world like ours who is able not to worry? Besides, we are not birds of the air or flowers of the field. Neither birds nor flowers have the higher sense in which worry takes root. I do not want to be a bird or a flower. I cherish the sensitivities and the loves that can make me anxious. But I need a trust that will keep my worry subdued to go along with these sensitivities. Jesus does not tell me to be unconcerned with what my family will eat tomorrow and what they will wear next winter. God knows we need these things. What Jesus says is, Don't be distracted by these things from seeking God's rule in our hearts.

What do you do to keep anxious worry at a minimum? Consider the persons you know who at first sight have the most to worry about. Are they not frequently the least worried people? Why? Maybe, because they are so occupied with loving others, they have little energy remaining for self-centered anxiety. The person who is busy with deeds of God's love and mercy today will probably be the one to trust God's love and mercy to be sufficient also for tomorrow.

Matthew 6:24—God and Money

Some translations spell *mammon* with an uppercase *M*. That is because some people have made a god of their money. That is idolatry. And for Israel, idolatry was the foremost of sins. Jesus does not say that money is evil. He does not denounce the institution of private property. Serving money and the worship of wealth is what Jesus condemns. First Timothy 6:10 echoes this indictment from Jesus by saying, "The love of money is a root of all kinds of evil." Everyone loves money, except persons vowed to poverty. Jesus' warning should remind us, however, that money is a kind of drug. It can make slaves of people no less than other narcotics. Medical science has ways of analyzing human blood to determine the level of narcotic or poison in the person. Are there ways of analyzing the level of our love for money? How much does it dominate our life? What do we sacrifice for the sake of making and keeping more money? Is not each of us a battleground on which money and God contend for our souls?

The Son of Man has authority on earth to forgive sins (9:6).

THE HEALINGS
Matthew 8–9

DIMENSION ONE:
WHAT DOES THE BIBLE SAY?

Answer these questions by reading Matthew 8

1. What does the man with leprosy say when he kneels before Jesus? (8:2)

2. What does Jesus tell the man with leprosy after healing him? (8:4)

3. Why does the Roman centurion come to Jesus? (8:5-6)

4. What does the centurion ask Jesus to do? (8:8)

5. What does Jesus say about the centurion? (8:10)

6. What does Jesus then do? (8:13)

7. Who in Peter's family is sick? (8:14)

8. What prophecy does Matthew say Jesus fulfilled by this healing? (8:17)

9. What does the teacher of the law who came up to Jesus say to him? (8:19)

10. What does Jesus reply? (8:20)

11. What does Jesus tell the man who wants to bury his father first? (8:22)

12. When Jesus has quieted the storm, what do the men in the boat say? (8:27)

13. What do the two demon-possessed men in the region of the Gadarenes say when they see Jesus? (8:29)

14. What does Jesus do to the demons in the two men? (8:32)

15. What do the people who hear about it want Jesus to do? (8:34)

Answer these questions by reading Matthew 9

16. What does Jesus tell the man who is paralyzed? (9:2)

17. Why does Jesus tell the man to get up and walk? (9:6)

18. Why does Jesus say that he eats with sinners? (9:12-13)

19. Why do people not put new wine in old wineskins? (9:17)

20. What does the ruler want Jesus to do? (9:18)

21. What does the woman with the bleeding do? (9:20)

22. When Jesus restores the sight of the two blind men, what does he warn them not to do? (9:30)

23. When the crowds marvel at Jesus' healing, what do the Pharisees say? (9:34)

DIMENSION TWO: WHAT DOES THE BIBLE MEAN?

Three times in Matthew's Gospel we notice a significant pattern in Jesus' ministry related to a mountain: following a peak experience on a mountain, Jesus comes down to an episode of central importance to the meaning of his life.

In Chapter 4, Jesus is tempted on a mountain. After this meeting with Satan, Jesus makes the critical pronouncement of his preaching. He proclaims, "The kingdom of heaven has come near" (Matthew 4:17). In Chapter 17, when he descends from the Mount of Transfiguration, Jesus distresses the disciples with an announcement. Jesus announces that he is to be "delivered into the hands of men" and killed (17:22-23). And here in Chapter 8, in Matthew's account, after delivering the Sermon on the Mount, Jesus reveals that he has power and authority to heal. Not only does he have that authority, but he can cast out demons and forgive sins. In each case the mountaintop experience (deliverance from temptation, beatitudes, transfiguration) is followed by a demonstration of the gospel, the showing of messianic power and authority, and the prophecy of the Passion.

Chapters 8 and 9 form the narrative portion of Matthew's Book II. These chapters prepare the readers for the instruction and warnings to Jesus' disciples about to go on mission (Chapter 10). Like everything else in Matthew's Gospel, the chapters are carefully constructed. Three healings (8:1-4, 5-13, 14-17) are followed by two inquiries (verses 18-20, 21-22). Then come three miracles of power. The first miracle is calming the storm (verses 23-27). Next Jesus drives away the demons (verses 28-34) and forgives a man of his sins (9:1-8). The healings are interrupted once again by two more inquiries (9:9-17) before the chapter concludes with four more healings. The ten healings correspond to the Hebrew tradition that ten wonders were wrought for the ancient fathers in Egypt and ten wonders were wrought at the sea. This Gospel tells us that what Jesus does are the ten wonders of the new covenant. (Contrast Jesus' wonders with the ten plagues of God in Egypt. See Exodus 7–12.)

■ **Matthew 8:2-4.** People with many different skin diseases were called lepers. They were outcast from society. They were regarded as unclean and could not be touched.

(We have since learned that leprosy is not an easily communicable disease.) The man with leprosy does not ask Jesus to touch him. He simply confesses his faith, hoping that Jesus could make him clean. And Jesus does. Matthew intends us to recognize both compassion and power there. Note that Jesus is careful to obey the strict code of Israel. He tells the man with leprosy to go to the priest. "Testimony to them" does not mean proof that Jesus healed the man, but that the man had kept the code.

■ **Matthew 8:5-13.** Capernaum is a town near the head of the lake (Sea) of Galilee. This town is thought to be Jesus' home during his Galilean ministry. Unfortunately, the Gospels tell us almost nothing about Jesus' personal life. We do not know with whom or where he lived.

A centurion was a Roman officer in charge of a company of one hundred soldiers. They were, of course, the occupying forces. The Jews resented their presence intensely. When he hears of the paralyzed servant, Jesus announces that he will come immediately. But the officer surprises Jesus by saying, "Lord, I do not deserve to have you come under my roof." He implies that Jesus does not have to come. The healing will occur if Jesus simply says the word. Jesus had not found such belief in his power to heal in Israel. This story symbolizes Israel's rejection of Jesus as Messiah, while some in the Gentile world trusted the God of Israel.

■ **Matthew 8:17.** Matthew uses the Isaiah verse with reference to Jesus' healing ministry. The servant who takes away our diseases seems the logical figure with whom to liken Jesus. Isaiah 53:4 later came to be a messianic reference about Jesus' death on the cross.

■ **Matthew 8:18-20.** *Son of Man* is a title given to the redeemer who will come at the close of the age. According to Matthew, Jesus refers to himself frequently as the Son of Man. In Daniel 7:13, the title *Son of Man* is used in a radically different way. No one had ever forecast that the Son of Man would have nowhere to lay his head.

■ **Matthew 8:22.** What an abrupt and harsh word to speak to someone grieving for his father! And Jesus says this deliberately. Jesus here warns that no attachment, even the most sacred family obligation to bury the dead, can interfere with following him. The incident is too stylized to be taken as the way Jesus responds to the grief of one of the Twelve.

■ **Matthew 8:23-27.** Jesus' power over winds and waves is pictured here to show his dominion over nature. The key recognition in the episode comes in the disciples' wonder. They want to know what sort of man can command even the winds and the sea. The man who taught "as one who had authority" (7:29) now demonstrates that authority by healing (a sign of the Messiah) and supernatural sovereignty. These stories are told to emphasize Jesus' authority, not to get applause for the wonders themselves.

■ **Matthew 8:28-34.** In this incident, two severely disturbed men recognize Jesus as one who could disturb their mania. It was commonly accepted that, in the fullness of time, the Messiah would come and assert dominion over all demonic forces. The demon-possessed men perceive that the Messiah has come before the time. If they are driven out of these men, where would they live? They ask Jesus to send them into a herd of pigs. To the Jews, pigs were unclean animals, a fitting place to send the demons. To die in the waters was to return to the source of evil they had come from.

■ **Matthew 9:1-8.** If we want one episode that contained the essence of Jesus' Galilean ministry, none would be better than this. The narrative begins with the wonderful compassion and tenderness of Jesus (9:2). Immediately Jesus' gift of forgiveness is met by the hostility of the teachers of the law. The teachers of the law agree among themselves that Jesus blasphemes. Only God has power to forgive sins. When Jesus presumes to have such a capability, he is surely being blasphemous. Jesus reads their unspoken thoughts and accusations. He then challenges them with the question, "Which is easier?" However they reply, Jesus has the final answer in the encounter. He enables the paralyzed man to rise and walk home. Because he could do that (which no one but the Messiah would have been able to do), Jesus could also say, "Your sins are forgiven."

Matthew completes the revelation by saying, "They [the crowd that had witnessed the healing] praised God, who had given such authority to man" [that is; to humankind]. These last two words, to man, point beyond what the Son of Man has authority to do (verse 6) to the disciples and in Matthew's time to the Christian congregation.

■ **Matthew 9:9-13.** Who Jesus called to follow him and with whom he mingled could not have escaped anyone's notice. Matthew, called Levi by Mark (Mark 2:13), is a tax collector for Rome. What could have been more outrageous for a faithful Jew than to collect taxes from Jews for the Roman government? Moreover, the money was marked by an inscription to Caesar, which the Jews considered idolatrous. Jesus should not have associated with sinners, that is, with nonobservant Jews or with "pagans," those who worshiped other gods. By so doing he broke the ritual code of cleanliness. When challenged by the Pharisees, Jesus gave his unforgettable answer that he had "not come to call the righteous, but sinners." The chapter concludes with Jesus' raising the ruler's daughter, giving sight to two blind men, and restoring speech to one who was mute.

■ **Matthew 9:35-38.** This summary echoes what Matthew has already told us about Jesus (4:23). Matthew repeats that Jesus spends his time teaching in the synagogues, preaching the gospel of the Kingdom, and healing every disease and infirmity.

DIMENSION THREE: WHAT DOES THE BIBLE MEAN TO ME?

Matthew 8:1-17—Miracles

Do you have trouble believing in the miracles? If so you have lots of company. We modern people understand the world scientifically. That is, creation is subject to what we call natural laws. For many people, their world view allows no room for interruption of the familiar, demonstrable cause-and-effect order of creation. Creation would not, according to this view, suspend its order even for God. Or, as others might put it, God would not intervene in the "ordained" workings of creation. We can reconcile such a view with faith in God. After all, Christian faith does not depend on miracles. The only exception is the one supreme miracle of the Incarnation—God with us in the person of a suffering servant through whom we may enter into eternal life.

Two important things must be said both for those who believe the literal account of the miracles and for those who have trouble accepting them. A miracle is an event that evokes wonder and religious awe. A miracle leads beholders to give praise and thanks to God. We must never forget that the so-called miracles were signs pointing to the authority and power of God manifested in the Christ. Jesus never performed a miracle for its own sake, either to prove anything or to astonish onlookers. Quite the opposite. He says to the ones who have been healed, "See that you don't tell anyone" (8:4) and "See that no one knows about this" (9:30). We have misunderstood the meaning of the miracles if we concentrate on their mystery and their magic. Whatever did or did not happen in these ten wonders, what matters is that God heals and God forgives.

We are wise if we avoid being dogmatic about what can and cannot happen in the worlds of nature and people. Scientific laws, through constant research, may change as we gain greater insight. If God is the Creator of the universe, then God can presumably intervene in any way that serves the divine purpose. What way has God intervened in your life? What has God done for you lately?

Matthew 8-9—What Has God Done for You Lately?

Look back over Chapters 8 and 9. Try to hear what the Gospel says to us through these stories. Look beyond the journalistic reporting of events that occurred on the Sea of Galilee, at Capernaum, and in the region beyond the lake. The wondrous thing is not that Jesus stilled a storm on the lake long ago. But the truth that makes a difference is that God, through the living Christ, can still our fears and quiet the storms that toss us about. The good news that makes a difference is not what Jesus did for a paralyzed sinner long ago, but how God forgives people here and now whose lives have been paralyzed by unforgiven sin. How can dead people be brought back to life, be born again? How can people blind to the wonders of God's love have their eyes opened through Jesus Christ? Should we read the stories allegorically as well as historically? Did Jesus intend for us to understand the miracles by transferring the wonder to God, and through God to ourselves?

THE CONDITIONS OF DISCIPLESHIP

Matthew 10–11

DIMENSION ONE: WHAT DOES THE BIBLE SAY?

Answer these questions by reading Matthew 10

1. Who were the two sets of brothers mentioned first among the twelve disciples? (10:2)

2. Where did Jesus tell the disciples not to go, and where did he send them? (10:5-6)

3. What five things did Jesus tell them to do? (10:7-8)

4. What did Jesus tell the disciples not to take on their mission? (10:9)

5. How would the disciples live while on their mission? (10:10)

6. What were the disciples to do when anyone would not receive them? (10:14)

7. When they were persecuted in a town, what were the disciples to do? (10:23)

8. Would the Son of Man come before they had completed their mission? (10:23)

9. Why would the disciples be treated as Jesus would be treated? (10:24)

10. What does Jesus say about the person who refuses to take the cross and follow him? (10:38)

11. What does Jesus say about losing and finding life? (10:39)

Answer these questions by reading Matthew 11

12. What do John's disciples ask Jesus? (11:3)

13. What does Jesus tell John's disciples to tell him? (11:5)

14. How does John compare with the least in the kingdom of heaven? (11:11)

15. Who does Jesus say John is if people will accept it? (11:14)

16. What do people say about John? (11:18)

17. What do people say about Jesus? (11:19)

18. Why does Jesus denounce Chorazin and Bethsaida? (11:20-21)

19. What does Jesus say will happen at Capernaum on the day of judgment? (11:23)

20. What does Jesus say to those who are weary and burdened? (11:28)

21. How does Jesus describe his yoke and his burden? (11:30)

DIMENSION TWO: WHAT DOES THE BIBLE MEAN?

To live within sight of a United States Weather Service signal tower on the American coast is to receive advance signals of oncoming weather. Although the sun shines at the tower location, sometimes small-craft, gale, or even storm warning flags will fly. The U.S. Weather Service knows what weather is coming six to twelve hours ahead of its arrival. In

43

a sense, Chapter 10 runs up warning flags of what lies ahead for Christ's disciples and for all the followers of Jesus.

Despite clouds on the distant horizon in Chapters 8–9, on the whole, the climate through those passages was fair. Compassion, healing, and popularity preceded, attended, and followed Jesus. Moving into Chapter 10, we immediately feel a weather change. Conflict, persecution, and the loss of life itself cast long shadows over the future.

Chapter 10 is a teaching or discourse section of Matthew. It takes the form of instruction to the disciples. Jesus is now preparing them for their mission. With only slight changes to allow for cultural differences, we can read the chapter as instruction to ourselves.

■ **Matthew 10:1-4.** Jesus chose twelve disciples. These twelve correspond to the twelve tribes of Israel and constitute the twelve who will judge Israel on the Last Day (19:28). Three other lists of the disciples appear in the New Testament (Mark 3:16-19; Luke 6:14-16; Acts 1:13). They are not exactly the same, but the principal names are on all the lists. The two sets of brothers head each list. Six of the names in Matthew appear nowhere else in the Gospel.

■ **Matthew 10:5-6.** Did Jesus intend the mission in his name to be so narrowly exclusive? If we take the last two verses of the Gospel to be authentic (28:19-20), or if we consider Jesus' response to faith that he found among the Gentiles, the answer is no. This mission began with twelve ordinary people; not rabbis, but fishermen. Is it any wonder that Jesus directed modest beginnings? Even a worldwide mission has to begin somewhere. The place for the mission to start, given God's covenant and promises with Israel, is with "the lost sheep of Israel."

■ **Matthew 10:16-33.** Here we see at least mild warnings of what is to come. (The great storm warnings, "suffer many things . . . and . . . be killed," first appear in Matthew 16:21.) Sheep among wolves, those who profess Christ flogged in the synagogues, followers of Jesus forced to testify, being betrayed by their families (10:36)—this is what the disciples can expect. They had to take Jesus' word for it. The first readers of Matthew's Gospel could see such things for themselves every day. They believed that Jesus was a prophet indeed.

■ **Matthew 10:39.** We shall say more about the paradoxes of the gospel when we come to the cross (Matthew 27). But the first incredible paradox of our faith is that "whoever loses their life for my sake will find it." How do we lose life to find it? The meaning here is probably wider than just physical death as a martyr. Jesus may also be saying that one who spends his or her own life in the purposes and causes for which Jesus gave his life will find a new life through God's Spirit.

■ **Matthew 11.** Chapter 11 begins Matthew's Book III of his Gospel. This section culminates in the incomparable Chapter 13 (parables of the Kingdom). The principal theme of Chapter 11 is the contrast and choice between acceptance and rejection of the Son of Man. The chapter falls into three divisions: the relationship of John the Baptist to Jesus (11:2-19), the woes upon the cities who reject Jesus (verses 20-24), and Jesus' invitation and promise to all who labor and are heavy laden (verses 11:28-30).

■ **Matthew 11:2-6.** Apparently Matthew needed to make clear who John was in relation to Jesus. If people were to accept Jesus as Messiah, Matthew (and Jesus) knew by the tradition that a forerunner must come first. Matthew reports Jesus' confidence that he was the Son of Man. John, the messenger, came before him. Each in a way confirmed the other.

According to Matthew, John the Baptist seems to acknowledge Jesus to be the Christ at his baptism (3:13-14). Now that John is in prison he does not seem so sure (11:3). Why? Perhaps because Jesus was not behaving like John expected a Messiah to behave. Perhaps John felt something more should have been happening. What was the Messiah waiting for? Jesus responds to the question by saying in effect, let John make up his own mind. He knows what the Scriptures say the Messiah will do (Isaiah 29:18-19; 35:5-6; 61:1-2). All these things are happening. What further wonders will take place? Jesus is the Messiah, John is the forerunner. Being sensitive to John's anguish and bewilderment in prison, Jesus tells John that it is enough that he is not scandalized by what Jesus does.

■ **Matthew 11:7-15.** John was the messenger before Jesus, yes. But in his ministry he was always pointing to Jesus. In fact, if people will believe it, John is Elijah! Elijah had to appear before the Messiah came. No one will believe the Messiah has appeared unless Elijah has appeared. Jesus lauds John for his work in preparing the way. But what further need did John have for disciples? Even the least in the Kingdom is blessed beyond even the greatest who came before. Some bands of John's disciples may have continued even into Matthew's time (about AD 80). But by that time their work should have been long finished.

■ **Matthew 11:12.** Jesus never spoke a more baffling word than this verse, if indeed he said it just as Matthew reports it, and that in itself depends on the translation. The 1984 edition of the NIV is essentially positive: "the kingdom of heaven has been forcefully advancing, and forceful men lay hold of it." The current 2011 edition says the "kingdom of heaven has been subjected to violence, and violent people have been raiding it." It has been frequently demonstrated that allegiance to Jesus as the Christ would and could provoke disagreement, anxiety, and violence and that the advance of his ministry required diligence, intentionality, and strength (as suggested by the first translation). The second translation seems to take the perspective that opponents are violent (as opposed to the focus of the forceful proponents) in the face of Matthew's nonviolent Kingdom vision. Either perspective could be true.

■ **Matthew 11:16-19.** Jesus is saying that John was rejected because he fasted. Jesus feels he is rejected because he feasts (especially with sinners). These are just excuses. The people refuse to accept the Kingdom from either of them because the people refuse to meet its demands. But, says Jesus, time and events to come will tell. What we do will be vindicated or proved right (justified) by what happens in the end.

■ **Matthew 11:20-24.** These verses are interesting. Among other things, they hint at wonderful things Jesus had done in Galilean towns that the Gospels do not record. In any case, how appalling that people could look right at heavenly wonders, hear the call to repent, and ignore them. Tyre, Sidon, even Sodom would not have failed to take advantage of such an opportunity.

■ **Matthew 11:28-30.** Here we come to one of the most consoling invitations and promises of the Scripture. Jesus offers rest to those who are weary and burdened. Who are these that are burdened? Surely Jesus speaks of the crushing load of laws grinding people to despair. "Come to me," says Jesus. "My burden (justice, mercy, and the love of God) is light." Jesus does not mean one can do it without strain. But his burden has lifting power that keeping hundreds of ritual rules does not.

DIMENSION THREE: WHAT DOES THE BIBLE MEAN TO ME?

Matthew 11:6, 21, 30—The Meaning of Being Jesus' People

Jesus sensed that John was offended, or at least put off, by the way Jesus was acting, supposedly as the Messiah. John preached the righteous wrath of God. Jesus came as a friend to tax collectors and nonobservant Jews. John was having trouble putting it together in Herod's dungeon. If Jesus was the Son of Man why was John allowed to languish so unjustly in prison? Jesus sent word, for what comfort it may have been, that if John was not scandalized by what Jesus said and did, he was blessed.

How often have we been scandalized by Jesus? Think back over just the portion of the Gospel we have read so far.

Don't some of the things Jesus has said offend our common sense? Are the meek really blessed? How are we supposed to resist one who is evil? How can we help but be anxious? And what about our traditional ideas of God's justice and mercy? Or even our own justice and mercy! Why should John meet death at the hands of a monster like Herod? Why doesn't the Son of Man have anywhere to lay his head? How are we to find our lives if we are to lose them? Unless I take up a cross and follow Jesus, am I not worthy of him? This seems like a lot to swallow.

And then Jesus tells us his burden is light! None of this makes much sense. It offends the spiritual fitness of things. And when we get to the cross, who is not offended by its outrage, scandalized that God would allow such a thing to happen? Jesus' word to John may well be a word to us.

Matthew 10:26, 28, 31—Do Not Fear

We have all kinds of reasons to have fear in our lives. We fear for our personal security. We fear for our health. We fear for the future of our world. We fear for our national defense. We fear for our social and economic structures to keep our high standard of living. Yet Jesus keeps saying, "Do not be afraid." If the living Spirit of Christ is with us, why do we have fear? Does Jesus who rules wind and wave rule the fears of the human heart? Why do we often feel the heaviness of our heart due to this fear?

The class may discuss this topic if time allows.

Matthew 11:30—The Easy Yoke

"My yoke is easy and my burden is light"? On the face of it, this seems incredible. But is it easy to take up a cross and follow Jesus? Is it a light burden to be persecuted for righteousness' sake? How can it be? Is Jesus being sarcastic?

We completely miss the point if we hear this as a promise to be excused from painful responsibility, or facing what Jesus faced. Disciples are not above their teachers. A yoke is a kind of wooden collar, part of the harness worn by beasts of burden to make the heaviness of their work more tolerable. Faithfulness to Christ is a kind of yoke that makes our Christian response easy. Not that we can escape from all that Jesus predicted in Chapter 10. But we can bear these burdens and face sufferings because we do not do it alone. God is with us. And to be part of the working out of God's purposes for the world is a yoke that gives new meaning to even the hard tasks that those purposes lay upon us.

Do we really believe that God is working all things together for our good? Even if it is suffering, can God use it to forward the divine purpose in our life?

Still other seed fell on good soil, where it produced a crop (13:8).

PARABLES OF THE KINGDOM
Matthew 12–13

DIMENSION ONE: WHAT DOES THE BIBLE SAY?

Answer these questions by reading Matthew 12

1. Why did the Pharisees rebuke Jesus in the grainfields? (12:1-2)

2. What did Jesus say David and the priests did? (12:4-5)

3. What did the Pharisees ask Jesus when he entered the synagogue? (12:9-10)

4. What did Jesus do for the man with the shriveled hand? (12:13)

5. What did the Pharisees do when they witnessed Jesus' act? (12:14)

6. What order does Jesus give the people he heals? (12:16)

7. What do the Pharisees say about Jesus when he heals the man who was blind and mute? (12:24)

8. How does Jesus answer this charge? (12:25)

9. What sin does Jesus say will not be forgiven? (12:32)

10. What three things does Jesus say he is greater than? (12:6, 41, 42)

11. What does an evil spirit do when he finds his house empty, swept, and in order? (12:45)

12. Who does Jesus say his mother, brothers, and sisters are? (12:50)

Answer these questions by reading Matthew 13

13. To whom does Jesus speak beside the lake? (13:1-2)

14. From where does Jesus speak? (13:2)

15. Where do the seeds fall in Jesus' parable? (13:4-8)

16. Why does Jesus say that he speaks to the crowds in parables? (13:13)

17. What does Jesus say to his disciples about prophets and righteous people? (13:17)

18. What is the meaning of the seed falling among thorns? (13:22)

19. What did the owner say to the servants who wanted to pull the weeds from his wheat? (13:29-32)

20. After the first two parables, what five similes does Jesus use for the kingdom of heaven? (13:31, 33, 44-45, 47)

21. In the parables of the weeds and the net, what will happen at the close of the age? (13:41-43, 49-50)

DIMENSION TWO: WHAT DOES THE BIBLE MEAN?

Winston Churchill called his first volume of the history of World War II *The Gathering Storm*. That would be a good heading for Chapter 12 of Matthew's Gospel. We saw the rough weather warnings in Chapter 10. Here the tempest openly breaks on Jesus. Then, as if to steady his hearers against the relentless beating of wind and wave, Matthew introduces the chapter of the parables of the Kingdom. The good news in these parables is like a strong anchor that has found the bottom beneath the threatening violence.

■ **Matthew 12:1-8.** Picking grain is considered work. Work on the Sabbath is prohibited. Faithful Jews must not violate the institution of the Sabbath. (See Exodus 20:8-11. The commandment about keeping the Sabbath is the longest of all the commandments.) Maintaining such ritual institutions as the Sabbath was one way Israel kept the faith in a sea of religious pluralism, which they found idolatrous and dangerous (even though they succumbed occasionally to it). So the Pharisees saw what Jesus did as a serious offense. The Sabbath had become encumbered with scores of rules and prohibitions. Keeping all these rules obscured every other care, notably hunger and healing. Jesus observes that if the priests could profane the Sabbath and still be guiltless, the disciples could feed themselves on the Sabbath. "Something greater than the temple is here" (12:6). The Son of Man has authority greater than the ritual of any institution.

■ **Matthew 12:9-13.** One could heal on the Sabbath only if life itself were in danger. Jesus and the Pharisees knew that the man with the shriveled hand was in no mortal danger. Jesus could have waited until sunset, the end of the Sabbath. He deliberately provoked the Pharisees in order to demonstrate that making people whole (mercy) took precedence even over ritual (Hosea 6:6).

■ **Matthew 12:14.** For the first time in his Gospel, Matthew reports critics of Jesus actually plotting to destroy him.

■ **Matthew 12:22-32.** Strong irony marks these verses. The unrestrained compassion of Jesus arouses the unrestrained hostility of the Pharisees. Because Jesus can bind the demonic domain of Satan, "the kingdom of God has come upon you" (12:28).

■ **Matthew 12:38-42.** An adulterous generation seeks for a sign. This means that faith is being prostituted to signs and demonstrations. (Remember the second temptation, Matthew 4:5-6.) The sign of Jonah was that Nineveh repented when Jonah preached. The sign of Solomon was that the Queen of the South came to listen. Now, Jesus is saying something greater than these signs is among them.

Jesus himself is God's sign. The poor in spirit, the meek, and the penitent need no other sign.

■ **Matthew 12:46-50.** Nothing here suggests that Jesus' family thought he was crazy. That notion comes from the incident reported in the Gospel of John (John 7:5). Nor must we infer that Jesus dismissed his family with a wave of his hand toward the disciples. The visit simply provides Jesus with the occasion to say that all who do the will of God belong to Jesus' family.

■ **Matthew 13.** A parable is a story that is used to teach some moral or religious truth and may or may not be true. A parable is used to make only one point. Good seed produces good fruit if it grows in good soil (13:8). In an allegory every detail carries some meaning for the illustration (verses 18-23). But in a parable the details themselves are important only as they point to the central purpose. Jesus also used the simile in his teaching. A simile is a statement of likeness in literal terms. For example, "The kingdom of heaven is like a mustard seed" (verse 31).

■ **Matthew 13:1-2.** Matthew is the only one of the four evangelists who incorporates these Kingdom parables into a single discourse. He does it in order to make them the teaching portion of his Book III. And he introduces them at this point in the Gospel in response to the accusations and challenges by the Pharisees, whom Jesus' ministry has provoked. From a boat Jesus addressed "large crowds" gathered on the shore. The disciples must have been among them, for, at least twice, he speaks specifically to them (13:10-17; 18:21-35). Sometimes we cannot be sure to what listeners all the words were addressed, crowds or the disciples.

■ **Matthew 13:3-8, 18-23.** The interpretation differs somewhat in purpose from the parable as first told. In verses 18-23, the parable becomes an allegory of the soils. These truths are no less pertinent now than they were then. To use the soils the word falls into as an allegory takes nothing from the original purpose. In 13:8, the purpose is stated that good seed produces a good harvest.

■ **Matthew 13:10-17.** Why parables? No other teacher, up to the time of Jesus, had used parables so extensively in teaching. They suited Jesus' purpose superbly on at least four counts. (1) *Parables made the truth specific and concrete.* Abstract and unfamiliar truth is made plain in terms of familiar, everyday pictures. (2) *Parables are unforgettable.* Jesus' purpose would be recalled whenever people encountered the common incident or simile that he used. (3) *Parables invite listeners into the scene.* The listeners then have to make their own responses to the reality that they find. (4) *Parables have polemical value.* Jesus used them to trap the Pharisees.

A parable, at first hearing, may seem to be about something far removed from the listener. Then the trap is sprung. Suddenly people find themselves locked into incriminating situations. They discover that the parable is about them. (The finest example of this in the Bible is the parable Nathan tells David in 2 Samuel 12:1-7. Read it again to see how effective such a simple story can be.) Among Jesus' parables, the sharpest polemical weapon is Matthew 20:1-16. The Pharisees perceived this parable as told against them.

Jesus never spoke in parables to conceal anything from anyone. Quite the opposite.

■ **Matthew 13:12.** Favoritism toward those already blessed seems unfair. But think about it. The more seriously a person takes the word of Jesus, the more that person will be able to get from it. The less another person cares about the things of the Spirit, the less the person will receive. Parallel truth can be readily seen with regard to musical skill, athletic ability, or language. From those who have not kept the gift once it has been given, even what they once had will be taken away.

■ **Matthew 13:24-30.** In Palestine there grew a noxious weed called *darnel.* In its early growth, it so resembled wheat stalks one could hardly tell the difference. To sow a man's field with darnel was a cruel crime. In this parable, Jesus likens the man who would do this to the devil, an enemy. Jesus told the parable as a way of saying that, in his proclamation of the kingdom of heaven, good seed has been sown. The opposition to this proclamation is poisonous and choking. At the end-time harvest, however, the good fruit will be gathered in to the kingdom of God. Later the church used this parable in facing the problem of backsliders in the young congregations. That illustrates how Jesus' parables serve more than one generation and setting.

■ **Matthew 13:31-35, 44-50.** Interrupted only by the explanation of the wheat and the weeds, the chapter closes with five similes (mustard seed, yeast, treasure, pearl, net). The tiny mustard seed becomes the greatest of shrubs, Jesus tells us. Jesus is not saying the great Kingdom came from such small beginnings. He is not pointing to the gradual growth of the Kingdom. Jesus is giving us God's assurance that the Kingdom comes.

And so it is with the yeast. The kingdom of heaven does not appear by gradually rising like bread. Through the yeast of God's word and purpose, the Kingdom comes.

The hidden treasure and the pearl of great value stress the discipline and sacrifice required of the disciples. But joy comes to those who find the secret of the Kingdom.

The chapter closes with the simile of the net. The end time will bring a harvest. Then the secrets of all hearts will be opened. Try to imagine what encouragement this brought to Christians under accusation, persecution, even crucifixion. In this good news they found hope!

DIMENSION THREE: WHAT DOES THE BIBLE MEAN TO ME?

Matthew 13:3-9—Even Good Seed Needs Good Soil

We have often moralized this parable about hard, rocky, and thorny soils. The original note of gospel has frequently been obscured. Jesus told the parable of the sower primarily to encourage the disciples who were going out to preach and teach. The good seed of God's word, sown in nourishing soil, brings forth an abundant harvest.

For teachers, parents, and all who in any way demonstrate the Christian life, this is good news. What does our parable have to say to us? In what ways are nurturing children and teaching others what it means to be a Christian hard and often discouraging work? How can we find comfort and courage in the assurance of good harvests somewhere beyond this time and this place?

Matthew 13:24-30—Letting Wheat and Weeds Grow Together

Few parables better represent the versatility and widely embracing relevance of Jesus' parables than this one about wheat and weeds. Jesus told it first to assure his listeners that harvest time would come. Evil might flourish now, but God would dispose of it at harvest time. Later, in Matthew's time, the parable was heard as counsel on how to deal with backsliders in the congregations. Should they be uprooted right away or do we wait until harvest time? We may hear the parable today with application to the broader question of dealing with evil in the midst of good. Do we have enough data and background information for gathering evil in the midst of good? When, in pulling up weeds, do we risk uprooting wheat as well? The parable poses the paradox of patience and zeal. When does patience sink into irresponsibility or indifference? When does zeal turn destructive of future good?

The class may discuss this topic if time allows.

Matthew 12:31-32—The Unforgiven Sin

No verses in Scripture have caused more anguish than these. They declare, "Blasphemy against the Spirit will not be forgiven." The verse implies everlasting guilt and torment for the person who speaks against the Holy Spirit. Sensitive persons naturally wonder if they may have spoken so as never to be forgiven. To be sure, Jesus says nothing about punishment for this sin. But remaining unforgiven by God would mean appalling spiritual condemnation. What did Jesus mean?

Look at the occasion on which the words were spoken. The Pharisees have just branded Jesus' healing as being of the devil. To call God's infinite mercy satanic reveals a heart, mind, and spirit utterly twisted and inverted. When a person deliberately or unintentionally denounces the goodness of God, that person has cut himself or herself off from God's forgiving love. Forgiveness requires that we be open to receive the healing acceptance of God. The person who, whether consciously or through indifference, cares nothing for God's presence and God's gifts should wake up to the state of his or her soul. How about you? Do you care enough about the things of God's Spirit to need and accept God's mercy?

"Who do you say I am?"... "You are the Messiah, the Son of the living God" (16:15-16).

7

YOU ARE THE MESSIAH

Matthew 14–16

DIMENSION ONE: WHAT DOES THE BIBLE SAY?

Answer these questions by reading Matthew 14

1. Why did Herod throw John the Baptist into prison? (14:3-4)

2. Why did Herod promise the daughter of Herodias whatever she desired? (14:6-7)

3. What did the daughter ask for? (14:8)

4. What does Jesus do when he hears about John's death? (14:13)

5. What does Jesus say to the disciples when they tell him to send the crowds away? (14:16)

6. When Jesus took the five loaves and two fish in his hands, what did he do? (14:19)

7. Where was Jesus when the storm arose on the Sea of Galilee? (14:23)

8. What does Peter say when he sees Jesus walking on the water? (14:28)

9. What do the disciples do and say when the wind stops? (14:33)

Answer these questions by reading Matthew 15

10. What does Jesus say "defiles" a person? (15:11, 18)

11. What kind of guides are the Pharisees? (15:14)

12. Who comes to see Jesus in the region of Tyre and Sidon? (15:21-22)

13. What does she want? (15:22)

14. What is Jesus' first response to the woman? (15:24)

15. Why does he finally heal her daughter? (15:28)

Answer these questions by reading Matthew 16

16. What does Jesus warn the disciples about the Pharisees? (16:6)

17. What does he mean by "the yeast of the Pharisees and Sadducees"? (16:11-12)

18. Who do the disciples tell Jesus that people say he is? (16:14)

19. Who does Simon Peter say that Jesus is? (16:16)

20. What does Jesus say to Peter? (16:18-19)

21. What does Jesus tell his disciples that he must endure? (16:21)

DIMENSION TWO: WHAT DOES THE BIBLE MEAN?

How ironic that Jesus should have come to Israel a contemporary of the monstrous family of Herods. According to legend, Herod the Great murdered the children of

61

Bethlehem for fear one of them would seize his power. He fathered seven sons by his five wives. He killed one of his wives. Of his seven sons, he murdered three. Two of his sons, first Herod Philip, then later Herod Antipas, married the same woman, Herodias. By levitical law (Leviticus 20:21) this marriage of Antipas to Herod Philip's wife was illegal. John the Baptist denounced him for it. Herod Antipas was a tetrarch, a petty ruler, over the region of Galilee. One does not denounce a despotic ruler without regret. To silence John, Herod threw him in prison. This was a frightful fate for one whose home was the desert.

At the vengeful request of his guilty wife, Herod murdered the Baptist. Herodias first used her daughter, the princess Salome, to pander to Herod's lust by her dancing. Then Herodias used Salome as a pawn to have Herod give her the severed head of the prophet on a platter. This murderer of John the Baptist later came to mock Jesus at his trial (Luke 23:6-12). What a contrast between the fear-ridden, lust-fired, power-hungry Herod and Jesus.

John's death must have sent a strong message to Jesus. If this is what happens to God's prophets, it will happen to God's Son.

■ **Matthew 14:13-21.** If you were asked to name the five most important events of the Gospels, what would they be? Certainly the Resurrection, the Crucifixion, and the Last Supper would head the list. From here on opinions would differ. Many people would include the feeding of the five thousand on any list of the key episodes of Scripture. Why?

The evangelists record the story of the miraculous feeding six times altogether. Such coverage is only given to Jesus' death and resurrection. If we regard the loaves and the fishes as a miraculous fast food service, its importance will seem exaggerated. But read the account carefully. Of what do the words "he gave thanks and broke the loaves . . . he gave them to the disciples" (14:19) remind you? (Turn to Matthew 26:26 and 1 Corinthians 11:23-24.) Such repetition of the words can hardly be coincidental. Almost beyond question, Matthew sees this story of the feeding as a foreshadowing of the messianic banquet that is to come at the close of the age.

One detail stands forth clearly. Jesus gave the bread and fish to the disciples to distribute. We can hardly miss the symbolism. Jesus transmits his comfort, his healing, his blessing through priests, ministers, deacons, elders, and faithful followers in the church.

■ **Matthew 14:22-33.** Once again Jesus demonstrates power over winds and waves. A further wonder attached to this storm is not found in the tempest in 8:23-27. Jesus walks on the water. We do not know how he did it. But what we have in this story is the good news of Christ's coming to his frightened and beleaguered followers in the church. The church has always been symbolized by a boat. In the midst of the storm Jesus comes across the water to the faithful saying, "Take courage! It is I. Don't be afraid." Of course, Peter sank when he trusted his own buoyancy. At least he dared to get out of the boat and try. Jesus' hand was there to catch him.

■ **Matthew 14:33.** "Those who were in the boat worshiped him." Matthew chooses the words carefully. There are several references of which others "worshiped him." But the references that the disciples "worshiped him" are only two in the Gospel of Matthew. The only other place he uses them is at the very end of his Gospel (28:17). When the disciples met the risen Christ on the mountain in Galilee, "they worshiped him." These words could properly refer only to the Messiah.

■ **Matthew 15:1.** Sending Pharisees from Jerusalem would be like sending in the FBI. This wandering rabbi is more than just a Galilean troublemaker. He spells trouble for the whole covenant people and nation in the minds of the elders.

■ **Matthew 15:2-20.** Jesus parallels the Pharisees' criticism of him with a sturdier condemnation of them. They ask, "Why do your disciples break the tradition of the elders?"

They mean by that the rabbis' oral or written interpretation of the law. Jesus comes right back with an even more severe accusation. "Why do you break the command of God?" Then in verses 4-6, Jesus pursues the attack even further. He asks which it will be, their tradition or God's word.

What really matters is what comes from a person's heart (15:18). What is in a person's heart is far more important than what goes into a person's mouth.

■ **Matthew 15:21-28.** Mark identifies the woman as a Greek woman of Syrophoenician birth (Mark 7:26). In any case she was not Jewish. Merciful though he was, Jesus has no thought of beginning the messianic age by a ministry to Gentiles. That would come later. Beginning with it would contradict every prophecy concerning the "lost sheep of Israel" that Jesus came to fulfill. Matthew's report, nevertheless, seems uncharacteristic of Jesus. His words are excluding. They lack compassion. Perhaps the exchange is presented this way to stress the unfaltering faith of the woman. Her faith is contrasted with the Pharisees' lack of faith. The incident reinforces the necessity of faith for receiving God's mercy. The story also dismisses the notion that racial or national boundaries can contain that mercy.

■ **Matthew 16:13-16.** The earliest Christian formula of faith was the affirmation, "Jesus is Lord." In most Christian confessions across the ages, the question asked at confirmations or professions of faith has been, "Do you accept Jesus Christ as your Lord and Savior?" According to Matthew, Simon Peter is the first to make this profession (16:16). Of course the Gospel from the beginning has left us in no doubt of who Jesus is. But now to hear it from the lips of Peter marks this exchange as one of the key revelations in the whole Gospel.

■ **Matthew 16:17-20.** We now come to probably the most controversial verses in the entire New Testament (16:18-19). These two verses have troubled readers for the last five hundred years at least and for centuries before that. What did Jesus mean when he said, "On this rock I will build my church"? The Roman Catholic Church reads it as Jesus' mandate for the papal succession beginning with Peter. Others read *this* rock as the faith that Peter has just uttered. On *that faith* Christ builds God's church. Still others see Peter not as the first leader of a worldwide Roman church but as the first to declare the faith that will constitute Christ's church. On all who follow Peter in his confession will Christ build the church.

Protestants, for the most part, do not think Jesus intended to make Peter and his successors the spiritual fathers of the church. Peter did become a powerful figure in the Jerusalem church following the Resurrection. Matthew may have been thinking of that church when he, alone of the four evangelists, introduces verses 18-19.

■ **Matthew 16:21-23.** Jesus' reprimand of Peter recalls his own dismissal of the devil after the desert temptation (4:10). To hinder Jesus in fulfilling his mission would be Satan's crowning achievement. This time he has used Peter as his disguised voice. And he chooses a most opportune time. Jesus has just acknowledged Peter's confession of him as the Christ. What could be more absurd than a Christ being killed by the elders and chief priests? So it seems to Peter, who rebukes Jesus openly. Nothing of this sort shall ever happen to Jesus. If Peter is the first to confess Jesus as Lord, he may also be the first to stumble over the fact that God is willing that his Christ die in the shame of the cross. Jesus saw it from afar. The disciples could not believe it.

■ **Matthew 16:24-28.** Not only will Jesus suffer and be killed. All who follow him, confessing his lordship, must also take up the cross, losing life in order to find it. This portion of the Gospel ends on a note of triumph: The Son of Man is to come in the glory of the Father.

DIMENSION THREE: WHAT DOES THE BIBLE MEAN TO ME?

Matthew 16:21—Christ and Suffering

If we think of the cross as martyrdom, as it has been for many, then we may not have to face it. To how many of us does the occasion come to be a martyr? But day by day (and this catches the essence of what Jesus meant) is another matter. Are we ready to live each day more concerned with others than with ourselves? Are we ready to go the second mile carrying whatever burdens there may be to lift? If anyone would be Jesus' disciple, would he or she not live in this way?

The class may discuss this topic if time allows.

Matthew 16:16—Who Do You Say Jesus Is?

This question calls not for a theological definition but for a personal response. What Jesus wants to know is who Peter thinks Jesus is and what Peter intends to do about it. No one can read the Gospel of Matthew nineteen hundred years later without running smack into this same question at the very heart of it. And what does it mean if we answer, "You are the Messiah, the Son of the living God," as Peter did? Our real answer may not be what we say with our lips. Our real answer is what we declare with our lives. Do we act as though Jesus has the word of life that can change hardness of heart into forgiveness and mercy? Do we behave as though the love of Jesus can break down dividing walls of hostility? Do I care enough for the people God loves to suffer with them and for them? These may be the questions that reveal who we really think Jesus is.

But many who are first will be last,
and many who are last will be first (19:30).

TRANSFIGURATION AND CHURCH DISCIPLINE

Matthew 17–19

DIMENSION ONE: WHAT DOES THE BIBLE SAY?

Answer these questions by reading Matthew 17

1. Who does Jesus take with him to the high mountain? (17:1)

2. Who appears to them when Jesus is transfigured? (17:3)

3. What does Peter offer to do? (17:4)

4. What does the voice from the cloud say? (17:5)

5. Whom does Jesus say was Elijah? (17:12-13)

6. What happens when the distraught father brings the boy suffering from seizures to the disciples? (17:16)

7. Why can the disciples not heal the boy? (17:20)

Answer these questions by reading Matthew 18

8. How can persons be the greatest in the kingdom of heaven? (18:4)

9. What should happen to ones who cause a little one to sin? (18:6)

10. What is God's will regarding these little ones? (18:14)

11. If someone who sins against you will not listen when you point out the fault, what do you do? (18:16)

12. If that person still refuses to listen, what then? (18:17)

13. What if he or she will not listen even to the church? (18:17)

14. How often should you forgive someone who sins against you? (18:22)

15. How much does the servant owe the king in Jesus' story? (18:24)

16. How much does the servant's fellow servant owe him? (18:28)

Answer these questions by reading Matthew 19

17. What does Jesus say about divorce? (19:9)

18. What does Jesus tell the disciples about the children who are brought to him? (19:14)

19. What question does the young man ask Jesus? (19:16)

20. What does Jesus tell him to do when he says he has kept all the commandments? (19:21)

DIMENSION TWO: WHAT DOES THE BIBLE MEAN?

■ **Matthew 17:1-8.** "After six days," continues the narrative. Those six days the disciples can never forget. The Gospel tells us nothing of what Jesus may have said to the disciples during those days. The last previous word we have is Jesus' announcement that he is to suffer many things and be killed. He also says that his followers must take up the cross and lose their lives for his sake. Six days is a long time to live with news like that without some further explanation. Maybe Jesus gave them one. But would explanations be enough? The crisis in the disciples' understanding called for an epiphany—a showing forth of God's glory in the face of Jesus (2 Corinthians 4:6). In the Transfiguration, that glory is shown to Peter, James, and John.

To help us understand the event, we need to probe what the word *transfigure* means. The word *transfigure* means literally to recognize in an object, person, or event a reality of another order, of a different kind. The appearance of the familiar is changed so that a new reality and meaning is revealed. Such a transfiguration of Jesus happens for the three disciples on the mountain.

By using our imagination when thinking about what happened before the Transfiguration, we will see that moment as God's endorsement of Peter's confession that Jesus is Lord and Jesus' revelation that he is to suffer and die. Now, in the Transfiguration, God says yes to these things.

This story contains images from the Old Testament. The images include Moses on Mount Sinai with three men (Exodus 24:9-18), the quotation from Psalm 2:7, three booths referring to the Jewish Feast of Tabernacles, and the presence of Moses and Elijah. Moses and Elijah also ascended to heaven as Jesus has done. God's pattern of revelation from the beginning is repeated here at a new summit.

■ **Matthew 17:14-21.** After the mountaintop experience Jesus and his three disciples must come down to the pain and difficulty of everyday life. A man cries desperately for help for his son with epilepsy who constantly falls into water and fire. The frustrated disciples cannot drive out the demon. To this scene of utter helplessness, Jesus comes down from being transfigured. He is disappointed to the point of aggravation with the disciples. The disciples are not successful because of their little faith. Jesus exaggerates in verse 20. Surely he does not expect people to literally hurl mountains all over the earth. What he means is that we face no difficulty beyond God's power to cope, whatever that may mean for us.

■ **Matthew 17:22-23.** Once again Jesus is in Galilee. He predicts for the second time the suffering and death that await him.

■ **Matthew 17:24-27.** We may overlook the importance of these verses. The sensational knowledge of the coin in the fish's mouth overshadows the more serious issue at stake here. The urgent question is whether faithful Jews can pay taxes to support the Roman temple of Jupiter. The two-drachma tax had been levied since the building of the second temple under Nehemiah. It was imposed by the Jews to support the temple. Later their conquerors imposed it. In Jesus' time the temple is still there. Of course, he and the disciples will support it. By Matthew's time the temple has gone. But the Romans still levied the tax. What were Christians to do? The episode seems to declare that although Christians are free, they live in a nation where taxes are assessed. As citizens, they are subject to that tax. Maybe Jesus is telling Peter to pay the tax from what he earns fishing. One fish with a coin in its mouth is not the answer.

■ **Matthew 18.** Here we have a manual of discipline for church members. To sense the importance of this chapter, imagine yourself a new Christian in the young congregation for whom Matthew writes his Gospel. You have been a faithful Jew, but you no longer find yourself at home in the synagogue. The congregation of Jews no longer welcomes you since you declared that Jesus is Lord. How will you live in the new community into which you have come? What rules will you live by now? What value does the young church have?

■ **Matthew 18:14.** Humility is the hallmark of the Christian. The ladder of advancement in the Kingdom goes down rather than up.

■ **Matthew 18:5-6.** Here is another conviction the young church lives by. But this one is quite out of the ordinary for the new Christian. Receiving a little child is the same as receiving the Christ himself. A community gathered in

Jesus' name will have a special care for the weaker members. In the weak ones will be the Christ himself at the mercy of the stronger ones.

■ **Matthew 18:7-9.** Jesus here has in mind the way in which one person, strong in faith, may cause a weaker person to stumble or sin. Not deliberately, but by careless insensitivity.

■ **Matthew 18:10.** "Little ones" does not always mean children. The term was widely used with reference to those new in the faith. Some translators use the words "common people." A community whose primary care is the insignificant nobodies is something new. The congregation must care for them as they would a child.

■ **Matthew 18:12-14.** In Luke 15:1-7, the parable of the lost sheep declares that God seeks a single lost soul as a shepherd searches for a single stray sheep. We do not miss that point here in Matthew. But this Gospel also stresses the responsibility of the community that no one be lost.

■ **Matthew 18:15-35.** The remainder of the chapter is a rule for church discipline. The requirement is for mercy and forgiveness. Yet the congregation itself must be protected. Verse 17 provides for expulsion from the community of any who refuse to listen and change their behavior. In verse 22, seventy times seven is a symbol of infinity.

■ **Matthew 19:3-12.** In a day when about half of all marriages end in divorce, these words of Jesus are troublesome. We cannot rationalize them to sanction our widespread acceptance of divorce: Jesus goes back to Genesis and God's purpose in creation (Genesis 1:27; 2:24) to show the sacredness of the marriage bond. Matthew (but not Mark or Luke) permits marital unfaithfulness as the sole ground for divorce. Moses also made an exception (Deuteronomy 24:1-4). With Mark and Luke there are no exceptions. Matthew's exception for unchasteness could have been added later to accommodate the people who could not keep the marriage bond until death. Interestingly enough, with Mark's report of Jesus' words, women and men are equally responsible when it comes to adultery in marriage. In any case, Jesus taught that marriage is a sacred bond that none were to break.

■ **Matthew 19:16-22.** Luke calls the young man a rich young ruler. He was not a political ruler, so far as we can tell. He may have been a teacher of the law. He was looking for a way to win eternal life. Jesus tells him to keep the commandments. This the young man has always done. So far, so good. Now Jesus lays the whole unqualified call for commitment on him. The commitment is too much.

■ **Matthew 19:23-30.** Jesus points out to the listening disciples how hard it is for a rich person to enter the kingdom of heaven. Wealth in itself is not the difficulty. The hold that riches have upon a person is the problem.

DIMENSION THREE: WHAT DOES THE BIBLE MEAN TO ME?

Matthew 19:9—Marriage After Divorce?

All laws in the United States say a person can remarry after divorce. Most churches allow a person to remarry even if the grounds of their divorce were other than unchasteness. What then do we make of Jesus' sweeping prohibitions? Are all people who marry after a divorce committing adultery? Even remembering that the social code that governed life in Jesus' day was quite different, it is still dangerous to take any of Jesus' words and make them mean what it is convenient for us to have them mean.

Let's assume for the moment that Mark and Luke (Mark 10:2-12; Luke 16:18) have the more accurate report of what Jesus said. Matthew's qualification, "except for sexual immorality," presumably was added later to accommodate to human weakness. Jesus probably said, No divorce. A generation or two later it became, No divorce, except . . . And that is what most Christians still say. The introduction of Matthew's allowance raises a new question. Which is the greater sin, living in an adulterated marriage, or divorce and a new marriage with new hopes? And how many ways are there to adulterate a marriage? Sexual infidelity is only one way. How does allowing other reasons for divorce violate the spirit or principle of what Jesus says in Matthew?

Even as we struggle with the question of which is the greater sin, we compromise the words of Jesus. We cannot deny that. Does our justification of compromise invalidate Jesus' central concern that marriage is a bond more sacred than any other we may assume?

The class may discuss this topic if time allows.

Matthew 18:32-33—If We Could Only Forgive Them!

Anyone who has ever had to forgive a great wrong knows that few things in all the world are more difficult. Who is sufficient for such a thing? Jesus' parable of the unforgiving servant offers help for such a need. The next time we have to forgive another person, instead of concentrating on the wrong done to us, suppose we were to think of the sum of all that others have had to forgive us. We may have disappointed persons who trusted us, we may have betrayed someone, or we may have failed to help someone who needed us. Think of all that God has forgiven us for. We have made idols of our possessions and achievements. We have not committed ourselves to making God's peace. We have passed by on the other side when many of God's little ones were hurt by the roadside. What debts and sins have we been forgiven? How can we say, If only we could forgive them?

*The Son of Man will be . . . mocked
and flogged and crucified (20:18-19).*

JOURNEY TO JERUSALEM

Matthew 20–21

DIMENSION ONE:
WHAT DOES THE BIBLE SAY?

Answer these questions by reading Matthew 20

1. With whom does the landowner make the agreement to work and for how much? (20:1-2)

2. At what later times after that does he hire more workers? (20:3, 5, 6)

3. Who is paid first, and how much do they receive? (20:9)

4. How much are those who worked longer paid? (20:10)

5. What complaint do the workers make who have worked all day? (20:12)

6. How does the landowner answer this complaint? (20:13-15)

7. Who comes to Jesus asking a special favor? (20:20)

8. What does she want? (20:21)

9. What does Jesus say in answer to her request? (20:23)

10. Why did the Son of Man come? (20:28)

11. What do the two blind men cry to Jesus as he leaves Jericho? (20:29-30)

12. What do they say to Jesus when he asks them, "What do you want me to do for you?" (20:33)

Answer these questions by reading Matthew 21

13. Where are the two disciples Jesus sends on an errand? (21:1)

14. What does he ask them to bring to him? (21:2)

15. Why does Jesus want to do this? (21:4)

16. As Jesus rides into the city, what do the crowds do? (21:9)

17. What is the first thing Jesus does when he enters the city? (21:12)

18. Where does Jesus go when he leaves the city? (21:17)

19. What does Jesus do on his way into the city the next morning? (21:18-19)

20. What do the chief priests and the elders ask Jesus when he enters the temple? (21:23)

21. What does Jesus ask the priests and elders in response? (21:25)

22. In Jesus' story, what is the difference between the two sons? (21:29-30)

23. What will the owner of the vineyard do to the wicked tenants? (21:41)

24. What do the chief priests and scribes think when they hear these parables? (21:45)

DIMENSION TWO: WHAT DOES THE BIBLE MEAN?

■ **Matthew 20:1-16.** This parable, at first reading, offends our common sense of fairness. Once we get into it with imagination it turns out to be one of the most gracious parables Jesus ever spoke.

The landowner in this case is the man who owns a vineyard. He has no labor force in his employ. He goes to the marketplace where laborers wait to be hired for a day's work. "Early in the morning" means sunrise. Notice that the first group is the only one with whom the landowner makes an agreement for a denarius. At nine o'clock, noon, and three o'clock he hires more workers. He must be trustworthy. These later laborers accept his word that he will pay them "whatever is right."

At five o'clock, he still needs help to gather his harvest. Perhaps he is trying to beat the oncoming rains. Not being hired was a dreadful thing for laborers and their families. They lived just a day's wages ahead of real hunger. The surprise comes when the men who have worked for twelve hours receive no more wages than the men who worked for only one hour. They take offense at such inequity of work for equal pay. The landowner counters their grumbling with the two questions in verse 15.

This parable is not about economics. What do you suppose would happen the next morning if the same man came to hire again? ("If we only work one hour we'll get the same pay.") This parable is about God's grace. Nobody gets one-twelfth of God's grace. God gives it freely to all people. Grace cannot be earned by hard work or long labor. The most recent convert receives the same as those who have stood within the covenant from the beginning.

■ **Matthew 20:17-19.** The Jordan Valley at its lower end lies more than twelve hundred feet below sea level. Jesus literally has to climb over three thousand feet to reach

Jerusalem. But we can also read "going up" as a metaphor. It means climbing to the summit of his life's mission, that is, to the cross. The large crowds that follow Jesus on his journey (19:2; 20:29) must not deceive the disciples as to the outcome when they get to Jerusalem. Mocking, scourging, and crucifixion await them. However, judging from the behavior of the disciples, they failed either to hear Jesus or to believe him.

■ **Matthew 20:20-24.** Comparing this passage with Mark 10:35-41 shows how Matthew softens the self-advancement of the sons of Zebedee. According to Mark, James and John themselves ask if they can sit at the right and left of Jesus in the Kingdom. Jesus later will denounce the Pharisees for loving the chief seats of the synagogue (23:6). How unbecoming of the disciples to ask for preference. Matthew must have sensed this. He puts the request on the lips of their mother. Mothers may be excused for wanting the best for their sons. Whoever may have asked the question, Jesus responded to the two disciples.

■ **Matthew 20:22.** Suffering fills the cup that Jesus asks them if they can drink. In saying they are able, they speak the truth. James was martyred by Herod (Acts 12:1-3).

The incident provides the lead for Jesus to speak about the nature of authority. The disciples must understand that greatness lies in serving people, not in lording it over them.

■ **Matthew 20:28.** The Greek word *lutron* (translated *ransom*) has enormous importance for the Christian faith. Christ died for us, and by his death we are redeemed. *Ransom* denotes the price paid for the emancipation of a slave. Jesus' death was voluntary. He accepted death on behalf of those who could not render sacrificial obedience on their own. A slave generally could not purchase his own freedom. The echo of Isaiah 53:11 confirms further that Jesus is the suffering servant of prophetic hope.

■ **Matthew 20:29-34.** The two blind men in Jericho cry out, "Lord, Son of David." (See also Matthew 9:27.) The crowds that go before Jesus into Jerusalem shout, "Hosanna to the

Son of David!" (Matthew 21:9). Clearly Matthew says, in the words of Zechariah 9:9, "See, your king comes to you."

■ **Matthew 21:1-11.** We associate the palm branch, the cross, and the empty tomb with the three most dramatic events in the life of Jesus. The triumphal entry (Palm Sunday), the Crucifixion (Good Friday), and the Resurrection (Easter Day) all occurred within the week that begins here in Matthew 21.

Between two million and three million Jews from all over the world customarily crowded into Jerusalem for Passover. Jesus chose this time to make his powerful declaration. Surely he was well aware how his action would be understood. The pilgrims would know their history. The people had cast their garments before Jehu when they made him king (2 Kings 9:13). Zechariah had promised that the king would come to Jerusalem riding on a donkey. They cried, "Hosanna to the Son of David!" a messianic greeting.

■ **Matthew 21:9.** *Hosanna* means literally "Save now." It was the people's cry for salvation from their enemies and from oppression. It has since come to be heard only as a shout of praise. "Blessed is he who comes" is a familiar greeting shouted to all pilgrims coming into the city at Passover time.

■ **Matthew 21:12-16.** Jesus wasted no time in going to confront the chief priests and scribes. He chose the temple itself to do that. Every faithful pilgrim was required by law to offer an unblemished animal or dove for sacrifice. The only place pilgrims could get these "perfect" specimens was to buy them in the temple precincts. Traders who were agents of the chief priests sold them for exorbitant rates. These merchants could victimize everyone who came to the Passover. The money changer charged a fee for exchanging the pilgrim's money into coinage so the temple tax could be paid.

Jesus was outraged. He thundered his denunciation by quoting Jeremiah (Jeremiah 7:11). He then turned the precincts upside down. What Jesus did in the temple that afternoon thrust him into a position from which he could not retreat.

■ **Matthew 21:15.** The children's cry probably echoed what they had heard the crowd shouting. Hearing the words coming from the lips of children gave Jesus the opening to refer to Psalm 8:2.

■ **Matthew 21:18-22.** This incident parallels Jesus' parable of the fig tree reported in Luke 13:6-9. Luke tells this parable as a warning that one who produces no fruit shall be cut down. Matthew introduces this parable on faith and prayer.

■ **Matthew 21:23-27.** "These things" refers to Jesus' defiance of the temple authorities. The priests and elders hoped they could trap Jesus into blasphemy. He escapes their snare by asking them a question they cannot answer without embarrassment, whatever they say.

■ **Matthew 21:28-32.** Jesus makes the meaning of this parable clear. The story stands as a commentary on 7:21-23.

■ **Matthew 21:33-43.** Jesus' parable follows closely that of Isaiah 5:1-7, where the vineyard of the Lord is the house of Israel. The tenants in Jesus' story violate the trust God gave them. They finally kill even the son and heir. The allegory is clear. Israel will not receive the inheritance. It will be let out to others.

■ **Matthew 21:45-46.** The three parables, the parable of the fig tree, the two sons, and the wicked tenants, all aim directly at the pretense and failure of Israel to repent. Israel has refused to hear, to obey, and to bring forth the fruits of righteousness. Of course the Pharisees perceive that Jesus speaks against them.

DIMENSION THREE: WHAT DOES THE BIBLE MEAN TO ME?

Matthew 20:1-16—Begrudging God's Generosity

One purpose of a parable is to draw the listener into the story. We learn from an experience in one setting of life to appreciate a truth in quite another realm. With whom do we identify in the story of the laborers in the vineyard? What do we learn from them?

Chances are most of us have identified with the workers who worked the longest. If not, why are we offended by the wages the landowner pays? But suppose we are among those hired at the eleventh hour. We have a family waiting for what we bring home if they are to eat tomorrow. What a joyous surprise, then, that the landowner is so generous. Should I refuse the denarius and ask him to give me only a *pondion* (a small coin worth two cents, one twelfth of a denarius)? But my family needs the food a denarius will bring.

I need all the grace God gives me. I should not judge God's generosity. Some people come late to the love of God. Shall I not rejoice that God loves us all without distinction of how lately we have come or how little we bring? And why not?

Give back to Caesar what is Caesar's,
and to God what is God's (22:21).

10
CONFLICT IN JERUSALEM

Matthew 22–23

DIMENSION ONE:
WHAT DOES THE BIBLE SAY?

Answer these questions by reading Matthew 22

1. What does Jesus compare the kingdom of heaven to in the parable? (22:2)

2. What do the invited guests do when they receive the invitation? (22:5-6)

3. What does the king then do? (22:7)

4. After the destruction what does he do? (22:9)

5. What does the king see when he looks at the guests? (22:11)

6. What does the king do to that man? (22:13)

7. How many are invited and chosen? (22:14)

8. What does Jesus say when the Pharisees ask him, "Is it right to pay the imperial tax to Caesar or not?" (22:21)

9. What do the Sadducees ask Jesus? (22:28)

10. What is Jesus' answer? (22:30)

11. What docs Jcsus say is the greatest commandment in the law? (22:37-39)

Answer these questions by reading Matthew 23

12. What does Jesus say people should do about the Pharisees? (23:3)

13. Why does Jesus say this? (23:2-3)

14. What does Jesus call the Pharisees? (23:13, 15, 23, 25, 27, 29)

15. What else does Jesus call them? (23:16, 17, 24, 33)

16. What does Jesus say is wrong with the Pharisees who give a tenth of their mint, dill, and cumin? (23:23)

17. How does Jesus compare the Pharisees to whitewashed tombs? (23:28)

18. What is the hypocrisy of the Pharisees toward the prophets and the righteous? (23:29, 30, 35)

19. What does Jesus say he would like to do to Jerusalem? (23:37)

20. What does Jesus say regarding Jerusalem? (23:38-39)

DIMENSION TWO: WHAT DOES THE BIBLE MEAN?

■ **Matthew 22.** Chapter 22 of Matthew tells of the continuing conflict between Jesus and his adversaries, the Pharisees and the Sadducees. The Pharisees and the Sadducees taunt, test, and try either to trap or silence Jesus. This chapter contains a parable, four controversies, and one more claim that Jesus is the Son of God.

■ **Matthew 22:1-14.** The Pharisees and chief priests must have found the parable of the king's marriage feast for his son the most offensive of them all. Its meaning is so unmistakable and unacceptable. A banquet always symbolizes the messianic feast of the age to come. The original form of this parable is in Luke 14:16-24. Notice that Matthew radically changed it. In Matthew, the banquet has become a wedding feast. (Does this symbolize the church, the bride of Christ?) He has the invited guests treat shamefully and kill the king's servants. (Could this be Israel's shameful treatment of the prophets and the Son?) The story in Luke lacks all the violence of Matthew's version. But both versions end with the people from the streets taking the places of the first invited guests who refused to come. (Is the invitation into the Kingdom now given to non-Jews?)

Matthew adds a second parable (22:11-14). This story is really a postscript to the wedding feast. One of the guests had no wedding garment. The word *friend*, with which the king addresses him, is really a rebuke, not a cordial greeting. Throwing a person into outer darkness seems a gross punishment for failure to dress properly. But in this parable the clothing the guest is wearing is a symbol of something far more serious than a dress code. One does not answer the Lord's invitation to the Kingdom wearing clothes of self-indulgence and careless devotion. The garments of repentance, righteousness, and praise are mandatory.

■ **Matthew 22:15-22.** The Herodians were what we would call collaborationists. Herod was subject to Rome. The Herodians therefore gave full allegiance to Israel's overlord. The Pharisees, on the other hand, hated Rome and the Roman violation of Israel's sovereignty under God. The Pharisees and the Herodians were strange allies. For different reasons, neither wanted Jesus stirring up trouble and subversion. They set a trap that could hardly fail to put Jesus on the defensive no matter what he said. Either he must offend the Herodians and Rome, or compromise Israel's highest obedience to God. His adversaries marveled at Jesus' answer.

■ **Matthew 22:29-30.** Another controversy was with the Sadducees. They were the conservative priestly party in Israel. Though small in numbers, they wielded great influence through Caiaphas the high priest. Jesus had acted with force against their operation in the temple. They sought to embarrass him with a question of case law (Deuteronomy 25:5-10). The case they proposed is preposterous. Seven brothers follow one another in succession into marriage with a woman widowed seven times, Whose wife will she be in the resurrection? The Sadducees did not believe in resurrection from the dead. The question was intended to make the idea of resurrection foolish. After his answer (Matthew 22:30), Jesus goes on to the principal issue of the resurrection. If God is the God of Abraham, Isaac, and Jacob, then the patriarchs must still live. If Jesus' opponents deny this they contradict sacred Scripture (Exodus 3:6).

■ **Matthew 22:34-40.** The fourth controversy centered on "the greatest commandment in the Law." Apparently Jesus' answer left no opening for rebuttal (Deuteronomy 6:5; Leviticus 19:18).

■ **Matthew 22:41-46.** The question in verse 42 appears to come from Matthew and not from Jesus. The argument is that if the Messiah were only a descendant of David, then David would not call him Lord. Matthew quotes Psalm 110:1. Such a contentious dispute over titles and their warrant does not sound like Jesus.

■ **Matthew 23.** Nowhere else does Jesus rise to such levels of condemnation and wrath as in these seven woes to the teachers of the law and Pharisees. No doubt Jesus had strong feelings against the Pharisees. We should keep three things in mind, though, to put the chapter in perspective.

1. When Matthew wrote this, followers of Jesus were under severe harassment and bitter attack by the Jerusalem Pharisees. The feeling, tone, and some of the abusive language of this chapter comes to us filtered through the later atmosphere of hostility.

2. The word *hypocrite* has a meaning for us today that it did not have in Jesus' day. For us it means one who wears a mask of pretense. A hypocrite wears a mask of feeling, piety, and righteousness that he or she does not really possess. In Jesus' day the Greek word *hupokrites*

meant one given to *casuistry*. We might call it niggling, fussing over minor details. They were excessive and mean-spirited about comparatively minor matters.

3. Jesus actually was sympathetic with what the Pharisees represented in Israel. They wanted to preserve the law and the disciplines of holiness. Notice verse 23:3. Jesus denounced the excess of petty obligations. These petty obligations crowded out "the more important matters of the law—justice, mercy and faithfulness" (23:23). A life consumed with observing rules has no passion for what the Lord requires above all else—acting justly, loving mercy, and walking humbly with God (Micah 6:8).

■ **Matthew 23:1-12.** These verses strongly echo Matthew 6:1-8, 16-18.

■ **Matthew 23:13.** Luke gives us the sense of these verses. "You have taken away the key to knowledge. You yourselves have not entered, and you have hindered those who were entering" (Luke 11:52).

■ **Matthew 23:15.** Converts often become extreme fanatics for their new beliefs. The Pharisees were not really seeking to lead people to God. They were seeking to lead them to be Pharisees.

■ **Matthew 23:16-22.** Jesus is condemning the way the Pharisees have of finding excuses from responsibility on a technicality. Jesus teaches his disciples not to swear at all (5:34). But if people do take an oath, it should be binding. Jesus' reasoning pulls the ground out from under the slippery ways of the Pharisees in avoiding obligation.

■ **Matthew 23:23-24.** To the Jews, almost all insects were unclean. Wine was filtered through muslin to strain out even the tiniest gnats. Jesus evokes a picture of a person swallowing a camel, another unclean creature.

■ **Matthew 23:27-28.** For a person to step on a tomb was to become fouled and ritually unclean. Tombs along a road were kept whitewashed so pilgrims and travelers would not accidentally step on them. Jesus uses the image of persons elaborately whitewashing the outside of their lives, while within they harbored "everything unclean."

■ **Matthew 23:29-38.** Abel was the first murder in the long history of Israel's sin. Zechariah (not the prophet) is mentioned in 2 Chronicles 24:20-22. (Second Chronicles is the last book in the Hebrew Bible.) The foul stain of murder runs through the long history of Israel. Jesus says there is a moral price to be paid. Lip service to the prophets will not pay it.

DIMENSION THREE: WHAT DOES THE BIBLE MEAN TO ME?

Matthew 23:29-36—These Who Murder the Prophets

People have frequently pointed out how hard it is to live with "saints." But we quickly elevate them to stained glass once they are gone and honor them with our devotion. Likewise with patriotism. Many who venerate Washington, Adams, and Jefferson might well have been horrified at their radical, revolutionary ideas had they been their contemporaries. In like manner, Jesus condemns the Pharisees because they "build tombs for the prophets and decorate the graves of the righteous," but lie in wait to kill the prophets the Lord sends now.

Do you ever wonder as you listen devotedly to the words of Jeremiah, Isaiah, or even Jesus, what you would have done had you lived in their day? More to the point, what do you do to those who come in their spirit today? Who are the modern-day prophets? Who comes to us in the name of the Lord?

The class may discuss this topic as time allows.

Matthew 22:21—Servants of God, Citizens Under Caesar

We marvel at how Jesus dodged the trap set by the Herodians and Pharisees. But the rule does not relieve anyone of the necessity of hard moral choices. We cannot in this life live in the pure realm of God's Spirit. To live in this world, social and political structures become necessary. We are citizens of communities and nations. Caesar serves as a metaphor for the order and authority of social institutions to which we are subject. At the same time, we are servants of God, bound by covenants of justice and kindness. In a very real sense we must live and move and have our being in two worlds at the same time. Living this way we soon make some painful discoveries.

Keeping the things of Caesar distinct from the things of God is not always easy. Nor should we expect to. We have to serve God not by withdrawing from the world, but through the institutions of our common life together.

Turning most of the moral decisions of citizenship over to Caesar is sometimes easier. Caesar keeps the social order. Let Caesar make the rules and call the tune. But if we do not believe that the state rules by divine right, then how do we render to God the things that are God's? How do we tell when to render to Caesar and when to render to God?

Whatever you did for one of the least of these brothers and sisters of mine, you did for me (25:40).

11

APOCALYPSE AND JUDGMENT

Matthew 24–25

DIMENSION ONE: WHAT DOES THE BIBLE SAY?

Answer these questions by reading Matthew 24

1. What does Jesus say when the disciples point out the buildings of the temple? (24:2)

2. What did Jesus say to his disciples when they asked, "When will this happen?" (24:4)

3. What did Jesus say must happen before the end comes? (24:7)

4. Because of wickedness, what will happen to the love of most? (24:12)

5. What else will happen throughout the whole world before the end comes? (24:14)

6. When are the people warned to flee to the mountains? (24:15-16)

7. What are the disciples to do when someone says, "Look, here is the Messiah"? (24:23, 26)

8. Will all these things happen before or after "this generation" passes away? (24:34)

9. How will the coming of the Son of Man be like the days of Noah? (24:38-39)

10. What will the faithful and wise servant be doing when the master comes? (24:45-46)

11. What does the wicked servant say and do? (24:48-49)

Answer these questions by reading Matthew 25

12. Why were five virgins foolish? (25:3)

13. What happened at midnight? (25:6)

14. What did the wise virgins say when the foolish virgins asked for oil? (25:9)

15. What did the bridegroom say when the foolish virgins arrived after the door was shut? (25:12)

16. How did the man going on a journey entrust his property? (25:15) .

17. What did the servants with two and five talents do with the money they were given? (25:16-17)

18. What did the servant with one talent do? (25:18)

19. With whom was the master pleased? (25:19-23)

20. What did those on the king's right do? (25:34-36)

21. When had they done these things? (25:40)

DIMENSION TWO: WHAT DOES THE BIBLE MEAN?

■ **Matthew 24.** Except for the appalling scene of the Crucifixion, Chapter 24 stands as the most frightful part of the whole Gospel. The dreadful predictions of suffering and distress sound so apocalyptic. (*Apocalyptic* is a word we have become familiar with in the nuclear age.) The chapter sounds apocalyptic because it contains a real apocalypse. *The Little Apocalypse*, as it has come to be known, is thought to include Matthew 24:5-7, 15-22, 29, 31, 35. (We can read an earlier rendering in Mark 13.)

The word *apocalypse* means "a revelation of hidden knowledge about the future." This kind of writing forecasts ultimate destruction of the world. God presides as judge at the end of the present age. God dismisses evildoers to the outer darkness, while the righteous are received into eternal joy and dwelling with God.

Apocalyptic writers believed the end of the age would shortly arrive. Terrible distress would assail even the faithful. But people were not to despair. God would gather the righteous to the kingdom of heaven. They must stand firm. God will not abandon the faithful. The best known apocalyptic writings in the Scriptures are the Book of Daniel in the Old Testament and the Book of Revelation in the New Testament.

Jesus shared the first-century Jewish viewpoint that God would bring history and the world to an end. But his emphasis was not on when or how the end would come. Jesus emphasized that people should be ready (Matthew 24:42, 44, 46; 25:1-13).

■ **Matthew 24:2.** By the time of Matthew's Gospel, Jesus' prediction of the final destruction of the temple has already happened. Not one stone was left upon another! Factional fighting among the Jews and the battering Roman forces have destroyed the city.

■ **Matthew 24:3.** Moses gave the law from Mount Sinai. Jesus delivered the Sermon on the Mount from a mountain in Galilee. So Jesus now speaks his final discourse from the Mount of Olives. Despite his warning against seeking signs (12:38-39), the disciples still asked for signs. Why? The mood of foreboding and fear was great. They probably could not resist the almost desperate need to know. Besides, Matthew needed a question to lead into the discourse on the end of the age.

■ **Matthew 24:5-8.** Whether the answer comes from Jesus or an anonymous writer of the apocalypse need not concern us. These verses are important because of the dreadful warning of horrors to come. And this is only the beginning. Indeed it was! Everything forecast here, and more, later did happen.

■ **Matthew 24:9-14.** Notwithstanding the dire predictions, things are not out of God's hands. Those who endure to the end will be saved. Christians were indeed facing frightful days. To hold on to their faith they needed a reminder that even those terrible times were still in God's hands.

■ **Matthew 24:15.** Daniel 11:31 and 12:11 speak of a desolating sacrilege. The reference is to the statue of Zeus set up in the temple by Antiochus IV Epiphanes, the Seleucid king who ruled over Syria in 168 BC. That was the sacrilege; the slaughter of swine added to the desolation. Two hundred years later, by AD 40, the desolating sacrilege was interpreted to warn that the Roman emperor Caligula would profane the holy place. He did. Now the apocalypse foresees further abomination ahead. "Let the reader understand" must be a reference to warnings that had already been given to Christians. This was their signal to flee to the east of the Jordan. In the ensuing siege and destruction of Jerusalem, the Jewish historian Josephus, who lived through the terrible events, estimated that over one million people died.

■ **Matthew 24:24-28.** The warning here is against being led astray by false christs and false prophets. In such times of hysteria, self-appointed messiahs and soothsayers prey on desperate people. But lightning does not flash for only a chosen few. Everyone will recognize the event of the Son of Man. No special kind of hidden knowledge will be required.

■ **Matthew 24:37-51.** The stress now shifts from dire prophecy to the need for watchfulness. The end is to come suddenly, no one knows when. The faithful must be ready. Jesus compares it to the way the Flood overwhelmed people who were unprepared at the time of Noah. Those who are ready will be taken. The others will be abandoned.

In verses 45-51, Jesus speaks in most characteristic fashion. In the meantime, the servants are to perform their duties faithfully. In all the time since then and now into the twenty-first century, the meaning of the parable has not changed.

■ **Matthew 25.** Three parables make up the final chapter of Jesus' teaching. These are the parables of the wise and foolish virgins, the talents, and the last judgment. We find each of them only in Matthew.

■ **Matthew 25:1-13.** The story of the wise and foolish virgins continues the theme of being prepared. Just as the foolish women rush to buy oil, the bridegroom goes into the house and the door is shut. When the tardy virgins finally show up with their oil, they are left out in the cold. The point of the parable is hard to miss. Those who do not plan faithfully, and wisely, for the kingdom of God while there is yet time, will not gain entrance when it arrives. There comes a time when it will be too late!

■ **Matthew 25:14-30.** The point of this parable is that God expects people to use the gifts they have been given. Not to use them (invest them) is to be unready for the master's coming when he asks "What have you done with that which you received?"

■ **Matthew 25:31-46.** The parable of the prodigal son (Luke 15:11-32) and this parable represent the summit of Jesus' teaching in parables. This story of the sheep and the goats combines eschatology (the belief in last things and God's final judgment) with ethical compassion (how we are to love and care for our neighbors). Such caring determines whether a person may enter the kingdom of heaven. Later the writer of the First Letter of John was to put it, "Whoever does not love their brother and sister, whom they have seen, cannot love God, whom they have not seen" (1 John 4:20).

■ **Matthew 25:31.** As in all apocalyptic literature, the Son of Man is here pictured as judge. But from verse 34 on, he is called King. In either case he is a messianic figure. The parable does not identify Jesus as the King, nor does Jesus assert his role as Messiah. The story stands unadorned by interpretation, a jewel in the world's sacred literature.

■ **Matthew 25:34-40.** The parable leaves no doubt that Jesus identifies himself with the hungry, the thirsty, the naked, the sick, the prisoner, and the lonely stranger. And how we respond to these persons is the true measure of how we respond to the Messiah. With this grand parable of moral judgment, the curtain falls on Jesus' ministry of preaching, teaching, and healing. Appropriately in the final picture Jesus becomes one with all who suffer. He has now to suffer his own humiliation and death.

DIMENSION THREE: WHAT DOES THE BIBLE MEAN TO ME?

Matthew 24:3-29—Apocalypse Now?

The descriptions in verses 7, 21, and 29 could be the scenario for a modern apocalyptic nightmare. But modern apocalyptic movies and literature, for the most part, do not see God as the agent of doom. Nor is there a vision of the gathering of the elect by the divine Savior (verse 31).

Is there any way that you see our modern predicament (and possible doom) as fulfillment of what was foretold long ago? Not that Matthew was literally telling our future. The writer of this apocalypse warned of the ruin of Jerusalem. But could such a fate be the justice and judgment of God? Remember Jesus' lament over Jerusalem facing destruction (Matthew 23:37). God would take no delight in a final judgment of the earth. But have we not eaten of the tree of the knowledge of good and evil (Genesis 3)? Have not the ways of death and life been set before us (Deuteronomy 30:18-19)? And is it not the choice of humankind to choose life or death? If we choose death, as Jerusalem did long ago, Jerusalem's fate awaits us. But there may be no recovery from the ashes of our fate!

The apocalypse of Daniel, Matthew, and John's vision of life and death in God's moral order may need once again to be reinterpreted for us today.

Matthew 25:31-46—Bad News and Good News of God's Judgment

Do we find any bad news in the parable of the last judgment? What good news do we find? Suppose we take the bad news first. Is it frightening that our entertaining the king of heaven depends on how we treat the weak, helpless, and miserable people of the earth? These are people we hardly ever need see or think about. We have no legal or political responsibility toward them. Our society is so structured that the hungry, the poor, and the homeless are for the most part kept out of sight and out of mind—until a moral reckoning is demanded before God and the Christ Spirit! Then the surprise of bad news. How are we doing?

What is the good news? Is it good to know finding the life promised by Jesus does not require some secret knowledge or some religious accomplishment? We find it every day in doing what we can for the least of Christ's brothers and sisters. How can we tell how we are doing? Look at our checkbook stubs, our appointment calendar, our list of friends and those who count on us. What things do we care most about in our life?

The class may discuss this topic if time allows.

Matthew 25:14-30—Have You Wasted God's Endowment?

The parable of the talents is another one of Jesus' parable surprises. This poor fellow who failed to invest the money his master gave him for safekeeping is hurled into the same outer darkness as the wedding guest in the improper attire. Does his "crime" call for such punishment? What is the parable saying to us? The parable is not about high-yielding investments, nor about talents such as musical skill or athletic ability. The parable is about what we do with the special gifts of God's grace that have been given to us.

What are the gifts of God's grace that have been given to you? Forgiveness, spiritual awareness, moral sensitivity? Does the parable not call us to ask, "Have I invested my spiritual and moral endowment to yield forgiveness among others, spiritual awareness among the disconsolate, moral sensitivity among the hardhearted?"

This is my blood of the covenant, which is poured out for many for the forgiveness of sins (26:28).

THE TRIAL OF JESUS

Matthew 26

DIMENSION ONE: WHAT DOES THE BIBLE SAY?

Answer these questions by reading Matthew 26

1. Why do the chief priests and elders not arrest Jesus during the feast? (26:5)

2. What happens in the house of Simon the Leper in Bethany? (26:6-7)

3. Why are the disciples indignant at the woman's sacrifice? (26:8-9)

4. What does Jesus say? (26:10-11)

5. What do the chief priests pay Judas for his betrayal? (26:15)

6. What meal do the disciples go into Jerusalem to prepare for Jesus? (26:17)

7. What does Jesus say as they are eating? (26:21)

8. What does Judas ask Jesus, and what does Jesus reply? (26:25)

9. What does Jesus do with the bread? (26:26)

10. What does Jesus say when he gives them the bread? (26:26)

11. What does Jesus say when he gives the cup? (26:27)

12. What does Jesus pray in Gethsemane? (26:39)

13. How many of the disciples watched while Jesus made this prayer? (26:40)

14. How did Judas betray Jesus to the crowd? (26:49)

15. What does Jesus say to the man who cut off the servant's ear? (26:52)

16. What do the disciples do? (26:56)

17. Why does the high priest tear his clothes during the trial? (26:65)

18. What is the verdict of the chief priests? (26:66)

19. What happens before the rooster crows on that night? (26:75)

DIMENSION TWO: WHAT DOES THE BIBLE MEAN?

With Chapter 26 we begin the Passion narrative of Jesus. This was the first part of the story of Jesus to circulate in the oral tradition. It was being told even before the writing of either Paul or Mark. The action moves through eight scenes.
■ **Matthew 26:3-5 (Scene 1—The Priests' Conspiracy).** The authorities had tried unsuccessfully before to arrest Jesus (21:45-46). Now the high priest himself, Caiaphas, joins the conspiracy to silence Jesus forever by killing him. But they do not arrest Jesus during the Passover. Too many Galileans, devoted to Jesus, are in the city for the festival. Caiaphas wants no riots, demonstrations, or trouble with Rome. But as soon as the pilgrims leave, the elders and priests will quickly execute "justice" and do away with Jesus.
■ **Matthew 26:6-13 (Scene 2—The Anointing at Bethany).** Neither Mark nor Matthew identifies the woman who

THE TRIAL OF JESUS

comes to anoint Jesus. John says the woman was Mary, sister of Martha and Lazarus, whom Jesus raised from the dead (John 12:1-8). Anointing could be associated with coronation of a king. It could also be a beautiful offering given to Jesus before his death and burial. At least one woman has some perception of what is to come.

■ **Matthew 26:14-16 (Scene 3—Judas's Conspiracy with the Chief Priests).** Ever since it happened people have wondered why Judas did it. The chief priests paid him thirty pieces of silver. Was money his motive? John implies that Judas was a thief (John 12:6). For such a pittance, would even a thief have stooped to what Judas did without further motive? Thirty pieces of silver is found in one of the prophecies of Zechariah (Zechariah 11:12).

Perhaps Judas was disillusioned. He may have hoped that Jesus would inaugurate the Kingdom. Instead Jesus talks about his humiliating death. Apparently he has no intention of leading a revolt to throw off the yoke of Rome. Perhaps Judas is jealous. He is the only Judean among the disciples. All the other disciples are Galileans, and to Judas they appear to be the favorites. Or perhaps Judas has done this to force the issue. Once Jesus finds himself under condemnation to die in disgrace as a Jewish heretic and a Roman criminal, surely then he will call on God to send "legions of angels" to deliver them all from Satan's power. How poorly Judas has understood Jesus if this is his motive. It seems unlikely that we will ever know for certain why Judas betrayed Jesus.

Judas probably told them of the place where Jesus could be taken under cover of darkness away from the crowds.

■ **Matthew 26:17-19 (Scene 4—The Preparation for the Passover).** The Jewish historian Josephus, a contemporary of Jesus, estimated that nearly two and three quarter million people were in Jerusalem for Passover. This guess is based on the number of lambs sacrificed for the feast. At least ten people could be counted for every lamb. Obviously one needed to plan to be there. Jesus left nothing to last-minute chance for this, the most important meal of his life. "My appointed time is near" was the code phrase that Jesus sent to the man whose upper room he had arranged to use for their Passover supper.

■ **Matthew 26:26-29 (Scene 5—The Upper Room).** Without question these are the best-remembered verses in all Christian literature. They were first written down in Paul's letter to the church at Corinth (1 Corinthians 11:23-26). Paul wrote this letter about twenty-five years after the Last Supper itself. The words had already become part of the liturgical practice of the early Christian churches.

Jesus realized that the upper room supper would be his last meal with his disciples. He wanted them to understand that his death was a sacrifice for all people in need of God's forgiveness. "This is my body" is Jesus' way of saying that he is dying for us. As we eat this bread we participate in his death. As we drink this cup, through his death, our sins are forgiven.

Jesus also intends that this meal, using the common elements of bread and wine found on every table, will become the opening of a new covenant between God and the new Israel. The wine symbolizes the blood that will be poured out in whatever way Jesus is to die. But it will not be just a victim's blood. It will establish a new relationship between God and the people of faith.

Jesus declares that this meal is the promise of the messianic banquet that the faithful disciples will enjoy with him "in my Father's kingdom." The promise of the Resurrection lies at the heart of that pledge.

■ **Matthew 26:3-56 (Scene 6—Gethsemane).** Verse 31 is a quotation from Zechariah 13:7. In this Gospel, the disciples did later meet the risen Christ in Galilee. Matthew reports such a prophecy here for that reason. Jesus tells the disciples that they will all fall away. Gethsemane (meaning "olive grove") lies in the Kidron Valley east of Jerusalem. It is on the lower slope of the Mount of Olives. We are admitted here to a most intimate and intense moment of life-and-death struggle within the soul of Jesus. We are tempted to refuse the cup of suffering that faithfulness to God requires that we drink.

That the crowd arrives with weapons indicates that the chief priests fear Jesus will start a riot of resistance. Twice before Jesus has used the word *friend* (20:13; 22:12) as a word of reproach. John says Peter struck off the ear of the servant of the high priest (John 18:10). Jesus' rebuke reminds the disciples that armed resistance is not the way Jesus is to go.

■ **Matthew 26:57-68 (Scene 7—The Trial Before Caiaphas).** Jesus was brought to trial twice. He was first brought before the Sanhedrin (high court of Israel). Then he was brought before Pilate, Roman procurator of Judea. The Sanhedrin needed to condemn Jesus in order to satisfy the Jewish laws prohibiting blasphemy. They needed to make sure that Jesus was punishable under their own system of justice and not just a victim of Roman justice. But the Sanhedrin needed the Romans to carry out the execution.

The Sanhedrin was presided over by Sadducean high priest Caiaphas. Apparently they wanted first to convict Jesus of blasphemy "so that they could put him to death" (verse 59). In Jesus' case, however, blasphemy might not have been enough to get a death sentence from Pilate. In Matthew 27, we see how the charge on which Caiaphas sent Jesus to Pilate was political subversion of Roman power.

For the Sanhedrin to gather in the middle of the night must have been highly unusual. Two witnesses had to corroborate each other for evidence to be entered. Caiaphas has much trouble with his hired witness. When he finally gets two witnesses to agree, he demands that Jesus testify on oath. He wants Jesus to swear that he is the Christ. Caiaphas probably would have said, "Tell us if you are the Messiah, the Son of God."

"You have said so" is taken to mean yes. What Jesus adds to the admission outrages the high priest. "From now on you will see the Son of Man sitting at the right hand of the Mighty One." That was the heart of blasphemy, to set oneself at the right hand of God! The Sanhedrin had the charge they needed according to their own system of justice.

■ **Matthew 26:60-70 (Scene 8—Peter's Denial).** Peter, alone of all the disciples, followed Jesus as far as the courtyard of the high priest's house. But having gotten that far, he denies that he even knows Jesus.

DIMENSION THREE: WHAT DOES THE BIBLE MEAN TO ME?

This Dimension Three is designed for use as a meditation. Will you reflect on the eight scenes you have witnessed through Matthew's words? Search your heart, memory, and imagination. By this exercise you can contemporize those events of long ago, feel yourself a part of the action, be chastened and reaffirmed in God's love.

Questions for Reflection

Have you ever arrested Jesus by stealth?
What have you ever done under cover of darkness, or anonymity, or in a crowd that would have hurt Jesus?

What beautiful thing have you ever done for Jesus in a time of great need?
You may be tempted to think at first, How could I do anything for Jesus? He's no longer here. But then you will remember "whatever you did for one of the least of these brothers and sisters of mine, you did for me." Like the nameless woman in Simon's house, did you ever make an extravagant offering to another person that was unsolicited, for which you could never be repaid, in which that person may have found grace and strength?

For what equivalence to thirty pieces of silver have you ever delivered Jesus to his enemies?

Was it your silent consent to some evil scheme because you did not protest? Was it your distrust of the ethics of Jesus when some hard choice was upon you? Was it your timidity to stand up and be counted for fear of what people would say?

Do you make Jesus welcome in your dining room?

What would you have to do to make your dining room fitting for Jesus? Would he think the room was pleasing to tired eyes and body? Would he enjoy the conversation at the table? Would he see how much you cared about the people who produced the food and prepared it? Would he see you eat with a thankful heart?

What meanings do the bread and the cup in the Lord's Supper have in your life?

What difference does it make to you to know that Jesus laid down his life two thousand years ago?

What does Jesus' prayer in the garden of Gethsemane tell you about your own prayers?

Where do you find faith to pray the second part of his prayer, not just the request, "May this cup be taken from me"? Where, if anywhere, is the spirit of Caiaphas alive in our world today? Where does Jesus threaten the comforts, privileges, and power of your life as he threatened Caiaphas's?

Of what denials of Christ would tomorrow's rooster crow remind you?

*Go and make disciples of all nations, baptizing them . . .
and teaching them to obey everything I have
commanded you (28:19-20).*

13

CRUCIFIED AND RISEN

Matthew 27–28

DIMENSION ONE: WHAT DOES THE BIBLE SAY?

Answer these questions by reading Matthew 27

1. What do the chief priests do when morning comes? (27:1-2)

2. What does Judas do then? (27:3)

3. What do the elders say to Judas? (27:4)

4. What do the elders do with Judas's money? (27:7)

5. What does Pilate ask Jesus, and what does Jesus reply? (27:11)

6. Who was Barabbas? (27:16)

7. What choice does Pilate give the accusers of Jesus? (27:17)

8. When the crowd cries for Barabbas to be released, what does Pilate do? (27:24)

9. Who carries Jesus' cross for him? (27:32)

10. What does the name *Golgotha* mean? (27:33)

11. What charge is fastened over Jesus' head as he hangs on the cross? (27:37)

12. What does Jesus cry from the cross? (27:46)

13. What does Matthew say happens when Jesus dies? (27:51-53)

14. Who watches the Crucifixion from afar? (27:55)

15. Who buries the body of Jesus? (27:57-60)

16. How does Pilate secure the tomb? (27:66)

Answer these questions by reading Matthew 28

17. Whom do the two Marys meet at the tomb? (28:2, 9)

18. What does Jesus tell the women to say to the disciples? (28:10)

19. What does Jesus tell his disciples? (28:19-20)

DIMENSION TWO: WHAT DOES THE BIBLE MEAN?

Many pilgrims in the late Middle Ages went to the shrine of Thomas à Becket in Canterbury. A moment of high exaltation came when they first saw the twin towers of the Cathedral far across the downs of Kent. Pilgrims journeyed toward the steps in the Cathedral beneath the tower where Thomas had been martyred. We come to such a vantage point today in our journey through Matthew. Before us rise the twin towers of Crucifixion and Resurrection, the very heart of the whole Christian gospel. Above and through those decisive events, we find the refuge and strength of God's Holy Spirit. These are the events, this is the revelation, toward which the Gospel has moved from the beginning.

■ **Matthew 27:1.** After the long night of interrogation, the chief priests and elders quickly decide how best to put Jesus to death. It immediately becomes clear what the Sanhedrin has known all along. Pilate the governor is the key person in their strategy of death. So, away to the governor's palace.

■ **Matthew 27:3-10.** Matthew is the only Gospel that tells what happened to Judas. The quotation in verses 9-10 comes essentially from Zechariah, not Jeremiah. Zechariah

11:13 tells how the shepherd of Israel has been treated with contempt. Such a small sum of money given for one sent from God can only be discarded. Judas probably never intended for things to go this far. The finger of judgment is also pointed at the chief priests. Knowing that Jesus is innocent, they cannot receive the blood money into the treasury.

■ **Matthew 27:11-14.** Matthew's account of the trial before Pilate is brief. It reveals little about how the charges against Jesus are advanced. But one point becomes clear if we set the earlier trial before Caiaphas alongside the trial before the Roman governor. Caiaphas hounds Jesus to death on the grounds of blasphemy. In Pilate's court the charge is political subversion of Roman rule. Pilate, who hated the Jews, could not care less about their religious squabbles. But keeping the peace, avoiding riots, and dealing swiftly with agitators who might challenge Roman power are important to him. The priests and elders play on the word *king* to appeal to Pilate's fears. Since Jesus does not defend himself, Pilate dares not turn Jesus back to his accusers where he might regain his freedom. Pilate is already in some disfavor with Caesar. More trouble here might finish him.

The Sanhedrin probably could not have executed Jesus on their own. Pilate might pay a terrible price if he refused to do it. Still, Pilate must wonder if Jesus is truly innocent. Pilate had no reason to trust the insistent accusations of the chief priests. Furthermore, Pilate also fears a miscarriage of Roman justice in sending an innocent man to his death. Tiberius Caesar would deal severely with such mishandling of imperial affairs. So Pilate tries amnesty as a way out of his dilemma. Releasing one prisoner at the time of festival was a tradition. We might call Barabbas a terrorist, doubtless condemned for breaking the peace or revolting against Rome. (Luke 23:18 says he was in prison for insurrection against Rome and murder.) Did Pilate privately hope that his accusers would ask for Jesus' release rather than the pardon of this folk-hero? No way this would happen! Was

Pilate troubled secretly by his wife's dream? In any case, he buckled under mob pressure.

■ **Matthew 27:24-26.** Pilate tries to wash his hands of all this. But, of course, he cannot. He is the one man in all Jerusalem who, even at this late hour, could stop this. Instead he joins them. So his name forever echoes in the Apostles' Creed—"He suffered under Pontius Pilate."

"All the people" (verse 25) refers not to all Jews. Rather it refers to the chorus of agitators hired by the elders to pressure Pilate into doing their will.

■ **Matthew 27:27-31.** Out of these five verses emerges a sickening picture of merciless mockery and Roman cruelty. The Sanhedrin orchestrated this hideous performance. The Roman soldiers play their music.

■ **Matthew 27:32-50.** The Romans added mental torture (27-30 and 38-44) to the physical brutality of crucifixion. They compelled the condemned man to carry the cross beam of the instrument of his death. The upright post was already planted at the place of execution.

Cyrene was a city of North Africa, the home of many Jews. Since Mark gives the names of two of the sons of Simon, he probably became a Christian. We find it intriguing to imagine that, in carrying the cross for Jesus, Simon became a follower. He is a pioneer and role model for many coming after him to carry the cross.

Death by crucifixion was death by humiliating torture. Nailed in a position causing excruciating pain, the victim suffered a thirst that often drove a man crazy. Jesus was exposed to the derision of the crowd. He was stung by flies and other insects. His body slumped forward to wrench every muscle and joint into unbearable contortion. Death often did not come for days. The crucified man was fortunate if a heart attack took his life quickly. It took six hours of this torture for Jesus to die. (Mark 15:25 says the Crucifixion began at 9:00 in the morning and that Jesus died at about 3:00 p.m.)

The only words spoken by Jesus from the cross, according to both Matthew and Mark, were those of Psalm 22:1. You should read the entire psalm in order not to hear this cry out of context. The final verses of Psalm 22 are a cry of confidence in God and praise. "All the ends of the earth / will remember and turn to the LORD" (Psalm 22:27). Can we be sure that Jesus did not have these words also in his heart as he died? I do not want to romanticize his death but want to recognize that the question of his devastation did not imply that he had abandoned his trust in God.

■ **Matthew 27:51-54.** This report is symbolic. The whole earth shakes at the cosmic impact of Jesus' death, "a new and living way" (Hebrews 10:20) opens through the curtain in the temple, and the saints are released from death by their resurrection.

■ **Matthew 27:55-56.** The women are the ones who watch with Jesus to the very end. The faithfulness of the disciples will be tested to the limits in days to come.

■ **Matthew 27:57-66.** The concluding verses of Chapter 27 serve two important ends. First, Jesus *died* and was *buried*! The Gospel leaves no room for the heresy that Jesus only appeared to suffer and die. Second, no human device or security could ever hold Jesus in the "agony of death," as Peter was to say in his Pentecost sermon (Acts 2:24).

When we move from Chapter 27 to Chapter 28, we step through a veil separating the public history of Jesus that everyone could see into the experience of vision and awareness possible only to eyes of faith. Unlike the Crucifixion, the Resurrection was not a public event. In fact, no one witnessed the Resurrection itself. This was God's doing and it remains God's mystery. After the Resurrection, the risen Lord first met the women in Jerusalem. He then met the disciples on the mountain in Galilee. The soldiers, posted at the tomb, did not meet the Christ. The vision was not given to Caiaphas nor Pilate. But, to those who loved and served the Lord in faith, the risen Christ appeared. And still appears! This is the promise of the farewell verse in the Gospel according to Matthew. (See Dimension Three for further discussion of the Great Commission, Matthew 28:16-20.)

DIMENSION THREE: WHAT DOES THE BIBLE MEAN TO ME?

Matthew 27:2—Delivered Over to Pilate

Matthew 27:2 is a statement to ponder. The chief priests delivered Jesus to Pilate for the kill. Caiaphas and his cohorts either could not or would not do the dirty work themselves. But they were ready to let Pilate do it. Perhaps, more truthfully, to force Pilate to do it. By this delivery of Jesus to Pilate, the chief priests rightly earn the world's reproach and condemnation for all time to come. But let our censure be tempered by some careful self-examination. How often have you delivered Jesus over for crucifixion by someone else? by your failure to take responsibility in making moral decisions? by silent consent as another person is slandered or made the object of personal abuse or exploitation? by your refusal to stand up and be counted for Jesus when some decisive cause is on the line? Imagine this verse as the summing up of any person's life: "He or she delivered Jesus to Pilate!"

Matthew 27:50—Jesus Gave Up His Spirit

With these words Matthew describes the moment of Jesus' death. Mark says more simply that Jesus "breathed his last" (Mark 15:37). Matthew's words lead the imagination on to a deeper meaning of what Jesus' death means. Jesus may have died from exhaustion. But his death was a choice on his part to leave his life (and death) completely to God. He chose to give everything he had in love for God, whatever the cost. He made the choice long before, as far back as the temptations (Matthew 4). In the garden of Gethsemane, Jesus repeated his earlier choice when he said,

"Not as I will, but as you will" (26:39). Caiaphas delivered Jesus to Pilate. Jesus yielded his spirit to God. What a contrast is here! The one is self-serving; the other self-emptying. Such is truly the choice given to every person, to every church, to every people who take the name of Christ. They can deliver him to death, or yield themselves to the stripes through which God's healing can come.

Matthew 28:16-20—The Great Commission

We call these last five verses of the Gospel the *Great Commission*. They are indeed the mandate for the Christian mission. The words are also a great promise: "I am with you always, to the very end of the age." What words could be more reassuring for the Christian than these?

What other messages come to you out of these words? What does this claim mean to you? Is Jesus your authority when the going gets tough? Does his moral authority empower you to stand tough?

A Prayer on Finishing the Gospel of Matthew

Eternal God, who spoke in a distant time and a remote place through the life, death, and resurrection of Jesus, and who yet speaks from the pages of your evangelist Matthew, speak now to our faith through your Holy Spirit. Over a long, long trail, winding from a miraculous birth in Bethlehem to a glorious epiphany on a mountain in Galilee, we have, through imagination, kept company with Jesus. We have been blessed by his beatitude, cleansed by his forgiveness. We have marveled at his healing, been born anew in the compassion of his love. We have taken courage from his presence and found hope in his promises.

Enable us now to keep all these blessings, and ponder them in our hearts. So, loving you more dearly, serving you more truly, may we faithfully await all the days of your appearing; through Jesus Christ our Lord. Amen.

About the Writer

Dr. Robert E. Luccock served as a minister and was professor of worship and preaching, Boston University School of Theology, Boston, Massachusetts.

CPSIA information can be obtained
at www.ICGtesting.com
Printed in the USA
FSHW020539120521
81374FS